THE *SCIENCE* DELUSION

The *Science* Delusion

Why God is real and Science is Religious Myth

2nd edition

Peter Wilberg

First Published by New Gnosis Publications
www.newgnosis.co.uk
© 2008 Peter Wilberg
British Library Cataloguing - in - Publication Data

ISBN 978-1-904519-06-5

2nd Edition published by New Yoga Publications

© 2017 Peter Wilberg

Cover images:
Bishop George Berkeley, Einstein's blackboard, Edmund Husserl

Science *is* the new religion.

Martin Heidegger

Anybody who has been seriously engaged in scientific work of any kind realizes that over the entrance to the gates of the temple of science are written the words: 'Ye must have faith.'

Max Planck

CONTENTS

Preface

The aim of this work is not to defend any specific religious doctrines or dogmas, but rather to offer a timely counterpart to the wave of aggressive anti-religionism exemplified by Richard Dawkins' 'scientific' critique of The God Delusion. It does so by critically examining the supposed rationality of 'science' itself, showing that it is as much based on unquestioned assumptions and dogmatic beliefs – accepted entirely on faith – as the most 'fundamentalist' of religions. The words 'science', 'conscience' and 'consciousness' all stem from the Latin *scire* – 'to know' – a verb whose root meaning is 'to cut through'.

By 'cutting through' the countless common myths and delusions that make up our idea of 'science', as well as those that science itself fosters and is founded upon, this book offers a 'heretical' challenge to the quasi-religious authority and almost totalitarian hegemony that the scientific worldview wields in today's globalised Western media and culture – a culture in which deference to 'The Science' has become as automatic as deference to 'The Church' used to be in medieval Europe.

The sterile Eurocentric and Western debate between religionists and anti-religionists, religious 'theists' and secular or scientific 'atheists' about the 'existence' of 'God' leaves open the far more basic questions of what exactly is meant by 'God', indeed of what it means for anything at all to be or 'exist' and - last but not least, Heidegger's basic question of why it is that anything at all exists or existed – even in the form of a Supreme Being or a Big Bang. In particular however, I will argue also that the question of God's reality is not in fact a question of the 'existence' or 'non-existence' of some sort of supreme being, one that merely 'has' or 'possesses' consciousness as its private property. For what if God simply is consciousness – not a consciousness that is either the product of any localised thing (such as the brain) or the private property of any being, human or divine – but rather a universal consciousness of the sort recognised in Indian thought – one that cannot be reduced to the product or property of any thing or being that comes to 'stand out' or 'ex-ist' within it. Whatever your standpoint on the nature and existence of God however, The Science Delusion raises two important questions:

(1) why is it politically and culturally acceptable to question the rationality of religious belief in the existence of an invisible God, a belief shared by both Newton and Einstein, but politically and culturally 'incorrect' to question – as did both Newton and Einstein – scientific belief in invisible particles of matter or 'quantum' packets of 'energy'?

(2) what is religious 'fundamentalism' a reaction to? Is it that religious fundamentalists are just mad or bad, or are they just unconsciously reacting to the rise of a new religion – the religion we call 'science'? For despite its global authority – and in the absence of anyone to play the role of 'God's Galileo' – this is a religion whose own fundamentalist dogmas remain invisible and wholly unchallenged In 'secular' educational institutions – leaving large numbers of people to blindly accept what I call 'The Science Delusion'.

Introduction

For the time being we have to admit that we do not possess any general theoretical basis for physics which can be regarded as its logical foundation.

Albert Einstein

Imagine someone holding forth on biology whose only knowledge of the subject is 'The Book of British Birds', and you have a rough idea of what it is to read Richard Dawkins on theology. [Dawkins: 'The God Delusion']

Terry Eagleton

"We are all unknowingly indoctrinated into the religion of physicality ... It is not simply a matter of the modern habitual acceptance of television, computers, atomic power, and rocket travel ... It is the unconscious assumptions we make about the world which have largely been determined and reinforced by the development of scientific thought in the last few hundred years. It is in the texture of our consciousness: how we experience and view the very chairs we sit on and all the other solid objects we see and use; how we conceive of space, of our movement through it, and of the motion of external bodies; how we experience the passage of time; above all, how we feel ourselves to be isolated, physical-biological entities governed by the laws of matter, with our life and consciousness soon to be explained away by an edict from biochemists and cell biologists."

Roger S. Jones *Physics as Metaphor*

A typical 'science' news article of the sort that can be found in the press today began by announcing that "Researchers at the University of Oxford will spend 1.9 million pounds investigating why people believe in God. Academics have been given a grant to find out whether belief in a deity is a matter of nature or nurture." In other words, belief in a deity is no longer even considered to be a theological or philosophical question at all – that is to say, a question of *thought* – but is instead reduced to a matter for 'scientific' investigation to be determined by 'research' (and that within the parameters of a wholly unquestioned, unthinking and superficial dualism of 'nature' and 'nurture'). More frightening than this is the fact that *not a single critical eyebrow is raised* at the new, wholly unquestioned faith in 'science' of the sort that this type of 'news' reveals. That is why, in the context of the controversy surrounding the role of religion in today's world – and the ever more aggressive attacks on it exemplified by Dawkins' book on *The God Delusion* – it is well worth remembering the words of the German philosopher Martin Heidegger, namely that "Science *is* the new religion." He pointed out also that science is "...to a quite unimaginable degree, through and through dogmatic; dealing with un-thought-through conceptions and preconceptions."

The identification of rational thinking with 'scientific' thinking opens us to the danger that Heidegger warned of. This was the danger of *thinking* as such *disappearing entirely* – to be replaced by a wholly unthinking science or a wholly *unthought* opposition of 'science' and 'religion'. For the fact is that most people remain literally 'blinded by science', unable to see or to see through its quasi-religious nature and the unquestioned dogmatic foundations on which it is based. The reason why faith in this "new religion" of science should be so blind is that it is based on a completely mythical understanding of the true history and nature of modern science and of scientific 'explanations' of the universe – which actually have the character of *mythical* explanations themselves. *The Science Delusion* offers a brief description and critique of a number of commonly accepted myths concerning the nature and truth of science.

Though there is a large degree of commonality and overlap between all these myths (both the myths surrounding science and the myths it fosters) my aim is (1) to raise the reader's consciousness of these myths *as* myths, and (2) to philosophically 'cut through', deconstruct and undermine them - demonstrating that they are indeed part of a general delusion about the nature of reality.

To begin with I draw upon and describe the early philosophical roots of modern science. This is significant in itself. For whilst scientists such as Stephen Hawking may dismiss philosophy and theology out of hand as outmoded or 'dead', they forget that modern science had its roots in 'natural philosophy' – and that the earliest pioneers of today's science did not even call themselves 'scientists' but 'natural philosophers'. It is high time then, to rescue Philosophy, the *mother* of Science, from the arrogance and hubris of its child. For even a cursory examination of terms used in physics for example, reveals a wholly unconscious use of language resting on countless unquestioned presuppositions as well as claims that contain clear logical contradictions or rely on entirely circular forms of argumentation. Thus while physicists like Hawking may claim that "philosophy is dead", in reality it is the failure of modern science to question, on even the most elementary level, its own most basic *philosophical* presuppositions and dogmas that effectively makes it into a delusory *religion*.

Myth 1

Science is 'materialistic'.

Religion is 'idealistic'.

The terms 'materialist' and 'idealistic' are here used in a philosophical sense which will be explained and returned to in the course of this work. And though part of the 'delusion' of science is its belief that it has successfully replaced all previous philosophies (which indeed it has done as today's dominant and *de facto* global religion) it was an English philosopher – John Locke – who first set out the philosophical basis of what was to become known as 'The Scientific Revolution'.

What is extraordinary however, is that even today Locke is still seen as an 'empirical' philosopher – one who believed that knowledge should be grounded in verifiable experience. In actuality he laid the basis for what, in philosophical terms, is a wholly 'idealistic' concept of scientific 'knowledge'. For Locke's main claim to fame lay in affirming Galileo's most basic claim – namely that what was ultimately 'real' was only the quantitative, measurable properties of things. This implied that behind all the tangibly experienced *qualities* of actually or 'empirically' experienced phenomena lay nothing but abstract or 'ideal' quantities. Thus the experience of a quality such as colour came to be seen as a mere interpretation by the brain of some quantitative 'frequency' of what is called 'electromagnetic energy' – itself a purely ideal mental construct invented by science.

It took an Irish philosopher – Bishop George Berkeley – to undermine Locke's philosophical separation between the so-called 'primary qualities' of things (in reality nothing but measurable *quantities* such as density and weight) and tangible qualities (such as hardness and heaviness). And it took a German thinker – Edmund Husserl – to offer a wholly different conception of science. What Husserl called 'phenomenological science' followed Berkeley in totally rejecting the whole project of seeking to 'explain' experienced phenomena and their qualities as mere subjective 'effects' of abstract, physico-mathematical quantities.

What is regarded as the 'scientific revolution' then, turned common sense notions of reality on their head. Far from being 'materialistic', the essence of this revolution lay in treating the mathematical concepts and theories of science – its *ideas* – as something that was *more real than the very phenomena they were supposed to explain*.

Thus, as Edmund Husserl argued in his groundbreaking work on *The Crisis in the European Sciences* the idea that natural science is 'materialist' or 'empirical' is a con. For in actuality it substitutes: "…a world of idealities for the only real world, the one that is actually given through perception, that is ever experienced and experienceable – our everyday lifeworld".

Here Husserl follows in the footsteps of Bishop Berkeley, who first saw through the myth that science offers us a more trustworthy or 'solid' account than religion of our actual experience of the world. This myth was also questioned by Husserl's student, Martin Heidegger, who insisted, as Husserl had done, that: "Phenomenology is more of a science than natural science is" – phenomenology being an approach to science which explores our direct lived experience of the phenomena.

As for the myth of scientific 'materialism', as Berkeley so eloquently argued centuries ago, whilst we experience the sensory qualities of so-called 'material' phenomena – qualities

18

such as heaviness or lightness, hardness and softness, shape and texture, colour and sound – we never experience or perceive 'matter' *as such*. The myth that science is 'materialistic' is thus also connected to the long-standing but now entirely redundant *idea* of 'matter' itself – what might be called 'the myth of matter'. For whilst science still faithfully clings to the idea of matter – albeit now designating it as a pure quantity called 'mass' rather than some form of hard 'substance' – both relativity and quantum physics no longer see it as possessing even those most basic and measurable 'primary qualities' that Galileo and Locke first associated with it – admitting instead that, on a 'quantum' level, such 'things' as mass, momentum, energy, space and time cease to be separately quantifiable realities, and that even 'particles' such as electrons turn out to have the same non-localisable and unbounded *wave* character as light.

In this sense, science has, in effect, itself become, like Berkeley's, a type of *immaterialist* worldview.

But a further problem is that questions about the 'reality' of anything, including God and matter, tend to equate reality itself with *actuality* – ignoring the entire dimension of *potentiality*.

Yet all actual experiences begin as potential experiences. Thus the actual experience of seeing a ball coming towards us is accompanied by an awareness of potential experiences in a different sensory dimension – such as the kinaesthetic dimension of moving to catch the ball and the tactile dimension of feeling it in our hands. In his book, *The Dimensional Structure of Consciousness*, Samuel Avery argues convincingly that we only *see* something as 'physical' or 'material' because of a sensed potential for *touching* it and experiencing tactile qualities such as hardness or softness. But the idea that these qualities necessarily 'belong' to some invisible substance called 'matter' that lurks behind our sensory experiences is just that – not an 'empirical' or sensory experience but a pure idea – for no one can see or sense matter *as such* – which is supposed to exist *independently* of any dimension of subjective sensory experience. Instead, as Avery notes: "We experience visual and tactile perceptions that suggest a material substance existing independently, but its acceptance as ultimately real is *an act of faith*." [my stress]

What we think of as 'matter' is real only in the root sense of the word, being the divine 'mother' or *mater* of all things – a womb of potential sensory experiences. The understanding that matter has essentially to do with a realm of potentiality is not a new one but long recognised by philosophers.

Aristotle, for example, understood what we call 'matter' (Greek *hyle*) as essentially pure, unformed or formless *potentiality* and only its form (*morphe*) as *actuality*. From this perspective, the primary 'stuff' or matter of the universe (the *prima materia*) is itself no *actual* 'substance' in the way 'matter' came to be thought of, i.e. as made up of invisible 'hard' particles. Nor is 'Matter' anything that can be 'objectively' experienced. Instead it is simply a realm or womb of different *potential* forms and qualities of subjective or sentient *experiencing* – all latent or potential in a universal *source field* of experiencing which Berkeley identified with a universal and divine 'mind'. 'Matter' can thus be seen as the very mind of 'God', understood as a universal or divine *awareness* of every potential pattern, quality or shape of experienced phenomena.

This universal 'mind', 'mother' or 'matrix' of all experienced phenomena however, contrasts radically with any mere 'matrix' of abstract mathematical *quantities* of the sort that modern science regards as more 'real' than *any lived experience* of reality, actual or potential.

Yet if the true 'mother', 'mind' or 'matrix' of all things didn't quite literally 'matter', i.e. manifest itself as qualities of *tactile experiencing* (for example qualities of hardness or softness, weight and density) then there would *be* nothing that we could experience, let alone conceive of *as* 'matter' in the conventional sense, i.e. as a substance made up of invisible 'hard' particles. And the more abstract concept of 'mass' is turn is understood as equivalent to a particular state of 'energy' – one which can *appear* to take the form of particles rather than waves. Nevertheless the ghost of the old 'matter myt'h lingers on in elementary physics education, where it has been defined, for example, as "anything physical that can be touched", forgetting that 'touch' is a dimension of sensory experiencing – of *subjectivity* or *consciousness* – from which the existence of no 'objective', 'physical' or 'material' *substance*, can, as Berkeley showed, in any way be deduced.

Instead, and as Max Planck – the originator of quantum physics – also declared: **"There is no matter as such – mind is the matrix of all matter."** Indeed he went so far as to accept that:

"Everything that we talk about, everything that we regard as existing, presupposes consciousness."

Similarly, the physicist Werner Heisenberg acknowledged that what we think of as atoms or particles are essentially not facts or 'actualities' but expression of a dimension of 'matter' understood in a more primordial way – as a realm of potentiality:

"[T]he atoms or elementary particles themselves are not real; they form a world of potentialities or possibilities rather than one of things or facts."

Myth 2

Science 'explains' things mathematically.

Religion accepts them on faith.

The truth is that even the most precise *quantitative* measurements or mathematical theorems and equations cannot – in principle – 'explain' even the most elementary *qualities* of our actual 'empirical' *experience* of the world – qualities such as colour, density, texture, taste etc. Have you ever seen, felt or touched or in any way experienced a quantity such as '3'? By this I don't mean a quantity *of* something – 3 oranges or stars, 3g of powder, 3ml of a liquid, three metres of carpet or road. I mean a pure, wholly abstract and immaterial quantity. In modern physics the only things that exist are such immaterial mathematical quantities, constants and relationships.

Yet even such a thing as 'mass' is *no longer* understood as a quantity *of* something tangible – like some sort of dense corporeal matter we could touch and feel – but as a pure, immaterial quantity. As a result 'mass' is a concept defined entirely by its mathematical relation to *other quantities* – such as velocity, momentum and acceleration – none of which themselves are ultimately quantities *of* anything whatsoever!

Thus when laymen ask scientists such questions as what 'mass' or 'gravity actually *is*, they are told this can only be 'explained' through a mathematics so complex and esoteric only the high priests of physics can understand it, one which should not be assumed to bear any relation at all to our actual experience of the world or even to the common meaning of words such as 'mass', 'gravity' etc. Instead, we are indeed expected to accept these concepts *on faith* and through a *priestly hierarchy* – exactly the accusation levelled against religion.

"That science is a religion and scientists its priests is often difficult to appreciate. If you are a layperson, you may believe in science and worship privately at its altar, but for the proper meaning and interpretation of events and phenomena, you must turn to the priest for guidance ... Although compassionate, the priest knows there is a limit to what the laity may receive. You cannot become fully enlightened."

Roger Jones

The much-vaunted *mathematical* precision of physics also goes together with a *looseness of language and logic* of a sort that would make any true 'rationalist' gasp with shock – the verbal answers and 'explanations' offered by even the most famous of physicists being so full of logical contradictions (or based on so many entirely circular arguments and circular definitions) that they would not pass logical muster even as high-school or undergraduate essays in that much maligned discipline called *philosophy* – a discipline of thought and precise use of language that physics and modern science as a whole just seeks to brush aside and marginalise, even though it was from *philosophies* of nature that the sciences first emerged.

Yet even laymen scratch their heads in the face of the most obvious logical and philosophical inconsistencies of scientific explanations – for example the inconsistency of declaring that time itself 'began' with the so-called 'Big Bang'. For it is self-evident that the very concept of a 'beginning' is itself a temporal concept and therefore one that already assumes the prior existence of time! If the very language of the scientific explanations is so loose and imprecise as to ignore *logic*, there is no way in which scientific claims – which are couched in words and not numbers – can be validated by even the most precise mathematics.

Science might mock religious ideas that we live in a universe created by an immaterial Spirit or spirits – but all it offers us in its place is the idea that we live in a universe of immaterial numbers! Its 'account' of the physical universe is just a set of mathematical numerical accounts in the *mind* of the scientist – quasi-mystical numbers that are then taken as supernatural realities – as semi-divine 'higher powers' behind nature itself.

And whilst, on the one hand, scientists argue that these numbers are based on actual measurements of physical phenomena, on the other they admit that they cannot actually say *what* exactly the phenomena they are measuring (mass, gravity, energy etc) essentially *are* – except as purely mathematical constructs or constants represented by quasi-mystical Greek signs and letters of the alphabet.

"It is an amazing fact about physics that none of its concepts are ever really defined. What we are given instead of a definition is a prescription for measurement ... Telling me how to measure space may make it possible to navigate in it, but it does not tell me what space is."

Roger Jones

Myth 3

Science is supported by hard facts.

Religion is undone by hard facts.

Were billions to be spent constructing the most sophisticated and expensive technological instruments and installations to detect ghosts, most people would consider this a most ridiculous, if not outrageous waste of money. Yet right now there are technical installations all over the world, constructed or in construction designed to detect what are, in effect, no more than *mental constructs* invented by scientists to prevent physics from falling apart at the seams. Examples are the massive installations built at great cost to detect the 'gravitational waves' postulated by Einstein's theory of gravity or the 'gravitons' that are supposed to make up an otherwise invisible and undetectable source of gravity called 'dark matter'.

But what if even the concept of 'gravitational waves' itself is one of many abstract mental and mathematical constructs that *pre-define* whatever it is that physicists seek to detect or measure through their equipment? This procedure is rather like first *defining* what 'ghosts' are through some abstract and arbitrary quantitative measure – and then seeking to 'prove' their actual existence by constructing some form of equipment for 'detecting' ghosts constructed solely on the basis of this measure.

As for 'hard matter' – another abstract construct of physics – the only 'fact' is that without postulating this occult or *ghostly* form of matter there would be no explanation as to why the *whole* universe does not fall apart – why mega-velocity stars for example, don't just spin off into space and why every galaxy does not unravel like a spiral-coil firework not held together by string. Yet the claim that 'dark matter' is something that necessarily exists 'out there' *to hold the physical universe together* is a perfect example of how scientists need to come up with ever more occult concepts to *hold their mental idea of the universe together* in the face of facts – to prevent not the universe *but their own theories* from falling apart at the seams and flying off into space!

Myth 4

Science rests on 'empirical' evidence.

Religion rests on dogmatic belief.

We have already seen one major reason why science is not 'empirical', for it does not rest at all on the evidence of our actual sensory *experience* of the world but instead seeks to explain everything we naturally and sensuously experience as a product of 'supernatural' energies, waves, fields or forces – all invisible and abstract *quantities* that we cannot experience directly.

This brings us to another reason why science is not based on 'hard facts' – a very simple one. For the most fundamental 'fact' of all is not the 'objective' existence of a world 'out there' but an essentially *subjective* awareness and experience of *such* a world. For how do we know that anything or anyone at all exists? How do we know we exist for example? Because of an *awareness* of being. How do we know that the world exists? Because of an awareness of experiencing it. But that means it is *subjective awareness and experiencing* that is the most basic 'fact' of existence – not any 'thing' we are aware of or experience as an objective 'fact'.

So again, the most fundamental scientific 'fact', 'truth' or 'reality' is not *objective existence* but *subjective experiencing*. That does not mean, however, that the world 'out there' exists only in our 'minds' or 'brains' – although *this is the conclusion* that both quantum physics and brain science lead us to. It is a false conclusion however, for though *what* we experience may be experienced as 'in here' (like an idea in our heads) or 'out there' (like an object in space) *experiencing as such* is not something 'out there' or 'in here' – only *what* we experience and *how* we experience it.

Experiencing is 'no-thing', yet that does not mean it is nothing. It is, quite literally, everything. Which is why philosophers like Leibniz and Whitehead adopted a philosophy of 'panpsychism' (see Appendix 3) recognising that no thing is a mere 'object' of consciousness but rather an experiencing 'subject' of consciousness – one that merely appears to other subjects *as* an object.

Reality then is not a physical-scientific relation between objects in an 'objective' universe 'out there', but is essentially an *intersubjective* construction within a *subjective universe* of experiencing. Spelled out in another way then, this particular myth is a claim that whilst science can provide objectively and experimentally verifiable 'evidence' for its truth claims, religion - even if it does not rely on faith in dogma - can at best provide only unverifiable subjective *experiences* for its own truth claims (for example different types of mystical or emotional experience of God). This is the biggest of 'black holes' at the heart of that holiest of sacred scientific cows – the notion of 'objectively verifiable evidence'. For if we apply this notion to scientists themselves, then – like every other person in this world – they are in no position to provide 'objective evidence' for the experienced reality either of their own consciousness or of their own thoughts. How then, can any experiment ultimately provide objectively verifiable evidence for any scientific 'theory' or 'hypothesis' if the experiential reality of the very *thoughts* that first constituted those theories or hypotheses (let alone the very consciousness or 'mind' in which they arose and were *subjectively* experienced) is itself unprovable?

Images from brain scans show nothing but images and readings of brain activity – they are not *proof* of the reality of consciousness or subjectively experienced thoughts, emotions, dreams that different types of brain activity are supposed to 'correspond' to. The fact that a scientist writes a scientific paper that is read and understood by other scientists is no more proof – in science's own terms – of the *reality* of the thoughts expressed in that paper than is a declaration of love, or a cry of pain proof that there is such a thing as 'pain' or 'love'. The truth that science dares not even consider is that *whatever* the 'objective' results of its experiments, spelled out in scientific papers, these remain just that – papers. The reality of the conscious mental activity and thoughts that generate their subject matter in the form of scientific hypotheses and theories, proven or unproven, remain, in the last analysis, objectively unproven and unverifiable. Instead of being 'objectively' verified they are *inter-subjectively validated* – accepted in the consciousness, thoughts and minds of *other scientists* – who happen also to have the *unprovable* subjective experience of engaging in mental activity and coming up with ideas, theories and hypotheses.

With what double-standards then, does science set about seeking to study 'dreams' through 'objective' data obtained from brain-scientific research, knowing that no amount of such data will ever prove that any person ever subjectively experienced such a thing as a dream, a human emotion of any sort – or even a thought? The wholly unoriginal thought that has occurred to many – namely that science becomes totally unstuck in the realm of human subjective experience, being incapable *in principle* of proving the 'objective' existence (let alone 'explaining') such a thing as 'love' – only goes to show to what degree scientific thinking is *in denial*. That scientists cannot prove the 'objective' reality of even the most *basic elements* of their own human subjective experience (whether their own scientific thoughts, sense perceptions or emotional feelings) and that the most seemingly 'objective' of scientific experiments, instruments and readings themselves also belong to the realm of *subjective* experience – scientists do after all only know from their consciousness and subjective experience that they are thinking up an idea, making an observation, handling an instrument or carrying out an experiment – all these constitute nightmare thoughts that threaten to undo the entire modern scientific worldview.

The alternative thought they threaten it *with* is that *reality as such* may, in the last analysis, be essentially *subjective* rather than objective in nature – and that ultimately it is inter-subjectively validated – even among scientists themselves. For otherwise they would be led – by their own criteria of objective verifiability – to demand *proof* of each other's *subjective experience* – indeed their very *existence* as conscious beings – before even sitting down to examine one another's models, theorems or experimental results. Together then with its confusion of *causes* of phenomena with their reasons and meaning, we must point out a yet deeper confusion in scientific thinking – the confusion of 'evidence' with 'experience'. Since its very inception, modern science has been based on distrust of *direct experience* - not least what is termed 'the evidence of the senses' – for sensory perception, like thinking and feeling is itself a mode of qualitative, subjective experiencing. Today, thankfully, many of the serious, lengthy and elaborate 'experiments' set up to provide evidence to 'prove' what every normal human being already knows from everyday (subjective) experience – has become almost a standing joke. Yet the attempt of science to use such objective evidence not just to support but to *invalidate* the reality of human subjective experience – not least religious experience – continues. One may dispute an individual's *interpretation* of a powerful subjective experience, but the attempt by modern science to use 'objective' evidence to disprove the *reality* of any human being's subjective experience is also dehumanising in principle.

Myth 5

Science has a logical foundation.

Religion does not.

This particular myth is not just one I have rhetorically inserted through the words of Einstein with which this book begins: "For the time being we have to admit that we do not possess any general theoretical basis for physics which can be regarded as its logical foundation." It has to do also with the very words 'logical' and 'logic' – together with their reflection in the nomenclature of the sciences (bio-logy, geo-logy, cosmo-logy) is rooted linguistically in the Greek word *logos* – meaning 'account', 'speech' or 'word'.

Yet scientists rarely even consider, let alone seriously question, their own words and verbal accounts of reality – which rely on their loose, inconsistent and highly metaphorical uses of everyday language. Instead, like Biblical fundamentalists they take their scientific terms and accounts for granted as *literal* expressions of truth – based on the myth that just because a word or terms like 'matter' or 'energy' exists, there is necessarily some existing 'thing' corresponding to those words. And no sooner has a new word or term been coined or become common currency – the term 'quanta' for example – that we take it as referring to some 'thing' that has always existed in the way that modern science understands it.

Few religionists or anti-religionists have yet realized that even the word 'religion' itself is a word of relatively recent coinage – yet having become common currency, we casually regard all faiths in all cultures and ages as varieties of this some 'thing' we call 'religion'– even though the languages of most non-Christian cultures and faiths have *no word* corresponding to the Latin based word 'religion' – which was a latecomer in Christian theological usage too.

The same applies to the word 'science'. It is somewhat tautological to dismiss the arcane beliefs, symbols and rituals of pre-modern cultures as 'unscientific' or 'pre-scientific' when the very notion of 'science' and 'scientific' truth is a *construct* of our 'modern' culture, and the very word 'science' – which originally meant simply 'knowledge' only goes back to the 12th century. Yet scientists have the arrogance to *privilege* the now sacred terminologies or 'Word' of science ('science-speak' or 'sciento-logy') over the languages of the senses, of literature and poetry, music and the arts – and mythology itself – denying *their* capacity to symbolise fundamental realities or truth. Ultimately the Greek *logos* is reduced to a set of purely mathematical 'accounts' of the universe, with mathematical 'logic' is set above language and seen as the highest, indeed ultimate parameter of truth – even though it is well-accepted that the foundation of mathematical logic itself lies not in any sort of evidence or measurements but in the supposedly *self-evident* truth what is called mathematical 'intuition', i.e. a form of subjective intuition.

A further paradox here is that what we take as the most elementary and intuitively self-evident mathematical intuition – for example that '1+1 = 2' - falls way short of the mathematical intuitions of religious thought. Thus many religions see God as 'One' and also as threefold or 'trinitarian' – describing God or the Godhead as a 'three-in-one' entity or 'triune singularity'. The basic equations or mathematical intuitions of these religions would be '1=3' and '3=1'.

A few moments reflection however, can show a far deeper *logical* sense to *this* mathematical equation than the everyday 'intuition' that '1+1 = 2'. For no 'one' thing can be perceived or conceived except in a particular field or context of appearance - which constitutes an implicit 'second'. The existence of any one thing then, automatically implies another – and therefore also implies a *relation* between this One (symbolised by the numeral 1) and that Other, symbolised by the numeral 2. This very relation of the One and its implicit Other however, constitutes a third term in itself – like the Holy Ghost in the Christian Trinity. The One [1], its implied second or Other [2] and their mutual relation [3]   may be distinct but they are also *inseparable* – and in this sense constitute a *higher unity* or Oneness [1]. So it is true: 1=2, 2=3 and ultimately 3=1 and 1=3! Yet not just simple arithmetic equations like '1+1=2' but much so-called 'higher mathematics' is based on artificially separating or 'abstracting' objects from their surrounding context or field of appearance – and then *counting* them as separate things or entities in a way which takes no *account* at all *of* that context – rather than truly *accounting* for how all things emerge *from and within* it a given field or context.

Myth 6

Science offers us an objective, physical understanding of the universe.

Religion presents us with subjective, metaphysical speculations.

The distinction between physics and *metaphysics* goes back to Aristotle and received new cogency through the insight of Martin Heidegger into modern science. What he reminded us of, quite simply, is that "Physics as physics can make no assertions about physics." Only a physics beyond physics or 'meta-physics' can. Why? Because "Physics as such is not the object of any possible physical experiment." And yet all the possible results of any physical experiment are already pre-determined in advance by the established constructs and framework *of* physics.

Yet since, as Heidegger points out, that very framework itself – "physics as physics" – is not itself the object of any possible physical experiment, nor can any of its theories ultimately be confirmed by a physical experiment.

The ultimate 'physical' explanation of the universe is of course the famous 'Big Bang' theory – a supposed event which took place who knows where, and 'before' which there *was* no such thing as either a space or time *in* which it could occur! And yet the illogical claim is made that the Big Bang can even be dated *in* time. But how can we 'date' the beginning of 'time' if 'dates' and 'beginnings' are themselves temporal concepts? And if space too, 'began' with the Big Bang where exactly could this even be said to have occurred? If the universe, time and space began with a Big Bang, are we not implying that there could be something 'before' time or 'outside' space?

It seems that such elementary logical and philosophical questions raised by this theory do not occur to physicists *as questions*. Yet these questions alone subvert the assumption that Big Bang theory is a verifiable physical hypothesis confirmed by physical evidence. Instead it is quite evidently a *metaphysical* theory in itself – loaded with metaphysical presuppositions – and a poor metaphysical theory at that - containing as it does the most obvious logical contradictions.

This brings us to the central myth of science itself – the myth of 'objectivity'. Modern science began by first assuming the existence of a world of independent 'physical' objects in space-time and then sought to explain the behaviour and relation of these objects. It saw these objects as external to and separate from the observer – even though neuroscience now tells us that the very objects we think that we perceive 'out there' in the 'physical' world are but figments or hallucinations generated and projected outward by the brain – which makes it somewhat difficult to 'explain' how the brain is supposed to first receive and interpret 'sense data' from these hallucinated objects!

Then again, the whole notion of external objects perceived by the brain or 'mind' through our body's 'senses' made no sense to begin with. It ignores the obvious truth that *all experiencing*, whether of ideas or objects, thoughts or things, is by nature *subjective*. Space itself, as Kant recognized, is not a basic dimension of objective reality 'out there'. It is a basic dimension of subjective experience, the subjective experience of things as separate from one another and from our own bodies.

Paradoxically however, despite having begun by seeking to explain objects and our perception of them, 'objective' science has, through quantum mechanics, removed the ground from under its own feet by ceasing to believe in the existence of 'objects' independent of a 'subject' – a human observer.

Whereas the Abrahamic religions raised God to the status of a supreme being or 'subject', both creating and ruling over man and creation, science has now raised man – as supreme subject or 'observer' – to the status of a supreme being or God. This is not a 'demythologization' of religion, but a new form of religious mythologisation – not of God but of man, and above all 'man' understood as 'scientist' – as an observing ego or subject standing over and apart from the universe rather than being a part of that universe. Again, Einstein was onto this delusion, which he correctly pictured as a type of imprisoning optical illusion:

"A human being is part of the whole called by us universe, a part limited in time and space. We experience ourselves, our thoughts and feelings as something separate from the rest. A kind of optical delusion of consciousness. This delusion is a kind of prison for us, restricting us to our personal desires and to affection for a few persons nearest to us. Our task must be to free ourselves from the prison ..."

The idea of a wholly *subjective* universe seems to be belied by our everyday experience of 'objects' such as tables and chairs, cups and kettles, computers and TVs, houses and trees. Yet if we think about it there is no such 'thing' as 'a chair' for example. Or rather, the telling word is the word 'as'. For when we think we are perceiving 'a chair' what we are actually doing is something quite different. We are perceiving some thing or 'phenomenon' – in essence a pattern of sensory qualities such as colour, shape, texture etc – *as* a chair.

What we think of as our most basic and reliable sense perceptions of 'objects' are in essence human *sense-conceptions* – for example our perception of something *as* 'a chair'. That is why an insect, however sharp its *sense perceptions*, would not and could not ever perceive 'a chair' – for it lacks the *idea* or *concept* of chair-ness. Animals do not perceive any of those things we take for granted as 'objects' existing 'out there' – things such as 'chairs'. Their worlds are not made up of 'objects' at all, but of subjectively experienced patterns of sensations of different sorts – such as colour, shape, smell, temperature or tactile feel.

That is why no amount of physical or chemical analysis of the thing we think of as 'a chair' will reveal anything to do with its 'chair-ness', since 'chair-ness' as such is not a perception but an idea or *conception* of something we perceive – even if that conception went into the very making of the chair. Our human conceptions of things as 'objects' have solely to do with our human world, with our human words for things, our specifically human relation to them and the specific human purposes for which we make or make use of them. It is we who, using it to feed a cat, both name and perceive something *as* 'a cat bowl'. A cat itself perceives no such a thing as 'a cat bowl'. Similarly, what makes the kettle in the kitchen 'a kettle' is no mere objective sense perception but our sense conception of it *as* a kettle. This sense conception of 'a kettle' has do with our human relation to it – in particular its sensed *potential* for being picked up, filled with water, turned on, and used to make a cup of tea or coffee.

This understanding of sense conceptions does not only apply to man-made 'objects'. For what in earlier ages human beings themselves perceived *as gods* – the Sun, Moon and Earth for example – are now merely perceived as 'bodies in space'. That is because they are scientifically *conceived* as such, and because it is scientific *sense-conceptions* that rule the day – that pattern our very perception of nature and the cosmos.

The difference between the worldviews and modes of perception belonging to religion and science is essentially a fundamental difference between their respective sense-conceptions. This is a difference that cannot be resolved by appealing to the 'evidence of the senses' or our everyday perceptions of 'objects' – for these themselves are shaped by our sense-conceptions. Nor can the difference be resolved in favour of the scientific world view by appeal to the concept of 'matter' or to the 'material' analysis of things. For 'matter' is itself a *conception* – one that expresses nothing *actual* or sense-perceptible, but rather the universal *potential* of things for being sensed, perceived, analysed, used and *conceived* in countless *different* ways.

Myth 7

Science shows that everything is 'energy'.

Religion believes that behind everything is 'god'.

Christianity has its dogmatic trinity of 'Father, Son and Holy Spirit' – all very human metaphors, including 'spirit' which derives from the Latin *spirare* – 'to breathe' (as in 'respiration'). Science has its own dogmatic quarternity – 'Matter, Energy, Space and Time'. The idea of 'brute' corporeal 'matter' was dispensed with long ago by a Christian – Bishop Berkeley, just as secular physics has now suspended it in favour of the paradoxical concept of matter as condensed 'energy', condensed 'space' or 'probability waves'. Today the great new dogma, shared by both science and new age pseudo-science is not the 'materialist' dogma that 'everything is matter' but the 'energeticist' dogma that 'everything is energy'. How did this theological revolution in the religion of modern science and in pseudo-scientific 'New Age' religions come about? Through scientific experiment or personal experience? No. For no one has or can ever 'experience' what is called 'energy' in the modern scientific sense – which is a mere abstract linguistic and mathematical construct. 'Energy' is one of the most central modern scientific terms that has become so common that, despite being 'no thing' at all, is still assumed by all to refer to an eternal reality or 'thing in itself'. Thus science speaks of 'electromagnetic' energy, theology of 'divine' energy, and New Age pseudo-science of subtle spiritual 'energies' of all sorts and an 'energy body'. In a word: 'Energy' is itself the 'God' of the new religion of science.

Yet just as few religionists ask themselves what they mean by 'God', so also do few scientists ever ask themselves what 'energy' *as such* essentially *is*. In its root Greek meaning the word refers to no 'thing' but simply to formative and transformative *activity* – its simple meaning is *action.*

Yet the tendency to think of 'energy' as some objective 'thing' and to turn that 'thing' into the essence of all things persists. Just as God continues to be seen as some supreme being or 'transcendental subject', so is Energy now seen as some supreme transcendental thing or *object* – one which, like God, is thought of as *lying behind all things* and as being their *ultimate essence and source.*

The revolution that overturned materialist science and has reached its apotheosis in the religion of 'Energy' had its roots in a circle of eminent scientists such as Helmholtz who sought to elevate and bring to dominance the concept of 'energy' and the so-called 'laws of thermodynamics' associated with it.

In his essay on 'Power vs. Energy – The Difference Between Dynamis and Energeia', Johnathon Tennenbaum shows clearly the geo-political use that the 'Energy' concept was promoted to serve:

"... the 'Energeticist Movement' associated with Wilhelm Ostwald around the turn of the 19th century advocated a World Government based on the use of 'energy' as the universal, unifying concept not only for all of physical science, but also for economics, psychology, sociology and the arts ... Not accidentally, the Kelvin-Helmholtz doctrine of 'energy' became a key feature of Anglo-American geopolitics, from the British launching of Middle East 'oil politics' at the beginning of the 20th century ... to a new Middle East war."

As Tennenbaum also points out, as a result of this Movement – and within the space of hardly more than a century – a veritable new religion or "cult of energy" has arisen. This is shown by the fact that millions of people now use the word 'energy' in all sorts of different texts and contexts, both 'scientific' and 'spiritual', as if its meaning was totally obvious. Yet at the same time not even the most advanced theoretical physicist in the world could actually answer the fundamental question of what 'energy' essentially *is* – or even admit to there *being a question here at all*. In the face of this wholly unquestioning use of the term 'energy', only a tiny few (Heidegger, Tennenbaum, Wilberg) have even dared to critically question it.

Myth 8

Science was a progressive revolution in our human understanding of nature.

Religion is reactionary, because it resisted and still resists this 'revolution'.

To dispel this myth we need to recapitulate the history and explore the nature of this supposedly 'progressive' scientific 'revolution'. The Greek philosopher Democritus was the first to give us an indication of what sort of 'revolution' this was and what its consequences might be.

"According to common speech, there are colours, sweets, bitters; in reality however only atoms and emptiness. The senses say to the intellect: 'Poor intellect, from us you took the pieces of evidence and with them you want to throw us down? This down throwing will be your downfall.'"

Fragment #125; Diels, 1992, p. 168; Dahlin's translation

As Dahlin comments:

"... Democritus was anticipating one of the fundamental difficulties involved in teaching natural science to children and young people today. This difficulty has to do with the "idealising" tendency of modern science, i.e. its reduction of our experience of the world to abstract representations and mathematical formulas in which the concreteness and contingencies of everyday life are annihilated, as it were – or at least set aside as belonging to the "not real". This has lately come to be regarded as a major stumbling block for students' learning in science."

In the fragment cited, the position still mythically attributed to Democritus himself – that everything is composed of atoms in a void – is treated sceptically by Democritus himself. For he clearly points instead to the paradox – and danger – of using an *abstract idea* of what lies 'behind' sensory experiencing to deny the *primary reality* of experience. In this way he foresaw what was to become known as 'the scientific revolution' – literally a delusory 're-volving' or total turning round of reality. This revolution or turnaround, as we have seen, first found clear and explicit expression in John Locke's philosophy of "primary" and "secondary" qualities.

In this philosophy all actually experienced sensory qualities such as colour, taste and texture are relegated to the status of "secondary" qualities and regarded as the (inexplicable) 'effects' of so-called "primary qualities". Yet in essence the latter were not *qualities* at all, but rather anything that could be reduced to a measurable *quantity*. This position of John Locke's was the one that Bishop Berkeley attacked most fiercely in defence of religion. He argued that since there was no way that we ever could *experience* Locke's measurable 'primary qualities' independently of the so-called 'secondary' ones, human experience was necessarily and self-evidently the *expression* of God – of a transcendental subject rather than a transcendental object or intangible 'thing in itself'. If Locke's position was that reality is only what is measurable, Berkeley's was that what was real was God – and God alone.

"… nothing can be more evident to anyone that is capable of the least reflection, than the existence of God, or a spirit who is intimately present to our minds, producing in them all that variety of ideas or sensations, which continually affect us, on whom we have an absolute and entire dependence, in short, in whom we live, and move, and have our being."

"That the discovery of this great truth which lies so near and obvious to the mind, should be attained to by the reason of so very few, is a sad instance of the stupidity and inattention of men, who, though they are surrounded with such clear manifestations of the Deity, are yet so little affected by them, that they seem, as it were, blinded with excess of light."

Bishop George Berkeley

Myth 9

Science has overcome 'The God Delusion'.

Religion still holds to it.

To question whether or not 'God' exists, and thus whether the idea of God is or is not a *delusion* begs a much deeper question – the question of how we understand what 'God' or 'Divinity' *is*?

Both religious *theists* and scientific *atheists* share a common idea of God as a *supreme being* – separate and apart from other beings and from the world. This theistic idea of God makes no sense, not only in scientific but in religious terms – for it reduces God to *one being among others*, and hence to a finite limited being. The idea of God as a *beginningless* being does not answer but *begs* the question of the origin of that Being – just as the scientific concept of time itself 'beginning' with a 'Big Bang' at a datable point *in* time does not answer but begs the question of what came before it.

Yet theism is only one among many different understandings of the nature of divinity. What if God is not a supreme or being but a supreme or ultimate *consciousness?* This brings us to what I see as the most important *delusion* shared by *both* science and religion. This is the delusion that consciousness or 'subjectivity' is the *private property* of a being or 'subject' – human or divine – or else that it is the mere *by-product* of some 'thing', whether matter or energy, bodies or brains. Along with this goes the false idea that 'consciousness' is identical with the elements that make up our conscious *experiencing* – or that of any being. What if it is not? What if consciousness *as such* is more like an infinite space or 'field' of pure awareness *within* which all experiencing and all experienced worlds arise? What if all beings – indeed all things - are but bounded and individualised portions of this pure, unbounded and universal awareness? This being the case, we might begin to see the *reality* of God in a quite different way – overcoming the delusory notion of God as some sort of supreme being 'with' awareness, and affirming instead that God, quite simply is awareness – not an awareness that is yours or mine, but one that is the very essence of the Divine. Behind both atheistic science and theistic religion is the failure to recognise that there can be nothing 'outside' awareness as such – beyond which there is nothing higher or more primordial.

Understanding God not as a supreme being but rather as a supreme *awareness* however, we can begin to acknowledge that we dwell within that awareness – within God – in the same way that we dwell within space, or that fish dwell within an ocean. An ocean is the *source* of all the fish and other life-forms that dwell within it, each of which is a unique portion and a unique expression of its source – the ocean as a whole. On this analogy however, religious theists are like fish that make the mistake of seeing the ocean as a whole in a purely *fishy* way – as one huge 'God-fish'. The religion of this theistic *fish* would then no doubt compete with that of other oceanic life-forms, who might see the ocean not as a supreme God-fish but rather as a supreme 'God-crab', 'God-octopus', 'God-whale', 'God-coral'. Getting fed up with such religious disputes, our dwellers in the ocean might decide that the ocean God was none of these things, but a purely indeterminate being or God that could not be represented as fish or whale, octopus or coral. They might become 'abstract' monotheists. Alternatively they might become 'polytheists', recognising God in the multiple forms of fish *and* whale, octopus *and* coral. As for *so-called* 'atheists', they would simply substitute the (poly)theistic idea of God as a Supreme Being in the form of a fish or whale, octopus or coral, with the no less religious idea of a Supreme Force, Supreme Energy, or, like Buddhism – a Supreme Void.

The current confusion that reigns in both science and religion is a confusion between *monotheism* and *monism*. The Abrahamic faiths are religious *monotheisms*. The chief religion of science is a quasi-religious monotheism of *man* rather than God, together with a *monism* that declares that 'Energy is Everything' and 'Everything is Energy'. Neither religious monotheism nor scientific monism have yet arrived at a fundamentally new way of thinking the nature of God and the Universe, one based on the principal that *Awareness is Everything* and that *Everything is an Awareness* – that all that can be experienced is an aware expression and portion of that ultimate, universal and unbounded Awareness that is the highest reality of all, that *is* 'God'.

I call this new monistic principle 'The Awareness Principle' – in contrast to 'The Being Principle', 'The Matter Principle' and 'The Energy Principle'. The Awareness Principle alone overcomes both the monotheistic 'God Delusion' (the delusion of a Supreme Being), and the monistic 'Science Delusion'. The fact that this Awareness Principle has yet to be acknowledged as *the* new foundational principle for science *and* religion rests on the most *fundamental delusion of all*. This is the delusion that 'subjectivity', 'awareness', 'sentience', 'consciousness' or 'experiencing' requires the *pre-existence* of an aware, sentient, conscious or experiencing 'being', 'subject' or 'self' – or can arise from a purely 'objective' and insentient universe of unaware things.

Myth 10

Science does not believe in miracles.

Religion does.

What greater myth unites science with theistic religions than the belief in the miracle of creation *ex nihilo* – out of nothing? The difference is only that whereas monotheistic religions see a single God as having created the world out of nothing at a datable time, science replaces this singular and divine *being* not with a singular and divine *awareness* but with what is termed a 'singularity' – in particular that singular point, from which – through the 'Big Bang' – everything (including time itself!) is supposed to have miraculously and inexplicably emerged out of nothing, also at a traceable and datable point 'in' time!

As theoretical physicist Paul Davies admits:

"Whatever the success of the big bang theory in explaining the key observed features of the universe, it is clearly incomplete. People always want to know what came before the big bang. Why did it happen at all? Here physical theory merges with philosophy and even theology ... Everyone agrees, however, that many of the deepest questions about our cosmic origins cannot be answered within the framework of existing physical theory. Hopes are pinned on a final unified theory that will merge all of physics into a single superlaw. Only then might we be able to answer the most fundamental question of all: why there is something rather than nothing."

The idea that a unified physical-scientific theory can address the fundamental philosophical question of why there is something rather than nothing is a contradiction in terms, since all scientific theories proudly assume to have their basis in the verifiable and measurable reality of some actual 'thing'. In answer to the unanswerable question of how the universe and time itself can be said to have begun at some datable time Davies refers to an alternative scientific model of an eternal 'multiverse'.

"In the 1960s, the ultimate origin of the universe was regarded as lying beyond the scope of science altogether, but today there are many attempts to explain it using physical theory, most often by appealing to quantum processes. If the big bang was indeed a natural event, then presumably nothing could prevent it from happening more than once. This suggests there may be many big bangs scattered throughout space and time, each producing an expanding universe of some sort. Possibly the entire assemblage of universes – often dubbed "the multiverse" – is eternal, even though each individual universe undergoes a life cycle of birth, evolution and perhaps death. In a popular version of the multiverse theory, called eternal inflation, universes 'nucleate' like bubbles in a liquid, and although each bubble universe may expand explosively fast, different bubbles are conveyed apart by unending inflation in the overall matrix of space faster than the bubbles themselves expand. As a result, the different universes rarely collide."

What exactly the *medium* is in which multiple universes 'nucleate' like bubbles in a liquid is left unclear. All we are offered is the philosophically loose and contradictory notion of big bangs "scattered throughout space and time" or "conveyed apart within the overall matrix of space" – when big bang theory itself tells us that not only time but *space* itself began with a 'bang' – space and time being inseparable aspects of 4-dimensional space-time.

There *is* a possible answer to the question of the medium in which multiple universes could nucleate. This is a wholly non-extensional or 'intensional' realm of *pure potentiality* – trans-spatial and trans-temporal – one brought to actualisation with ultimate trans-physical or divine *awareness* in the same way that an artist's very awareness of creative potentials allows them to differentiate and ultimately find actual expression. This however, is an answer that would not even be considered by physicists since it questions the scientific identification of reality as such with 'actuality' rather than potentiality, and its insistence on the fundamentally objective rather than *subjective* nature of the universe – or any multiverse.

Myth 11

Science has proved its truth through modern technology and medicine.

Religion has not.

Most people, unless they are engineers or scientists or have little or no in-depth understanding of how technical equipment and appliances of any sort actually work. They may remember a few ideas from school science lessons on mechanics or electromagnetism. They may have or recall a few ideas about the workings of cars and internal combustion engines, radio and TV, computers and smartphones, electromagnetic waves, as well as the electrical currents that provide energy to work their household appliances – but that is all. And yet these more or less vague ideas are enough to make them *believe* that modern science has proved itself through the effective working of all the technologies, appliances and gadgets it has given rise to.

Similarly, someone may have little knowledge of the Bible, but the ideas they have from it – or the miracles it describes – may suffice to make them believe all its stories – a belief encouraged by their religious teachers and the religious culture they might have grown up in. So if they happen to come across, for example, some archaeological discoveries that appear to disprove elements of these stories and how they came to be written, a certain state of 'cognitive dissonance' may arise which threatens to undermine their entire belief system. They may end up with questions that even their most learned theologians are unable to answer.

But rarely do we consider that the same thing applies to people who firmly believe in science on the basis of *its* technological 'miracles'. Indeed they would be very surprised to know that the highest theologians of this religion – physicists in particular – cannot even *define* the most basic ideas upon which its technologies are founded; they cannot even define what 'energy' is – or agree on how a simple 'electrical current' supposedly 'flows' through wires and makes electrical or electronic appliances 'work'. In fact the minute they would try to define how energy works their wires would get tangled and their brains would short-circuit. For since the most basic definition of energy is simply 'the ability to do work' they would have to confront the uncomfortable question of how an 'ability' can travel through wires or radiate through space, or how it can be transformed in the way different forms of energy are supposed to be transformed into one another.

From a strictly empirical standpoint – though we may feel warmth from an electric heater or see light coming from an electric bulb, we have no experience of any such thing as electrical or electromagnetic 'energy' *as such* – and therefore also no empirical experience of it 'transforming' itself into heat or light for example. Yes, we may get a shock if we touch a live wire. But again, not even the high-priests of the Science Religion can say what the 'electrical energy' that gave us this shock essentially is. And what sort of answer is it to say, as one of the most revered of such high-priests (Richard Feynmann) did, that 'energy' is "an abstract unchangeable quantity". A quantity of what? And if this quantity is so abstract and unchangeable that we cannot even say what it is a quantity *of* – then how does it 'do work', or make my household heater or vacuum cleaner or computer 'work'. Of course, there are simpler scientific ideas *about* 'energy' and how it 'works' – although most of these are also based on highly abstract mathematical theorems and ideas. We say these scientific ideas have been 'applied', that the result is all the energy-based technologies and technological equipment we have at hand which actually "work" – or at least have the "ability to do work" – which brings us back full circle to the conventional definition of energy itself!

In general, we need only probe just a little beneath the surface of any of the simplest, most basic and accepted *ideas* of the sciences, whether physics or biology and their applications, for example, in electrical engineering or medicine, to find ourselves in a quasi-theological realm of ghostly quantitative abstractions and obscure jargons bearing no relation to our qualitative, lived experience and perception of the world. Each specialist science is a vast edifice of such jargons – all of which are "idea constructions" (Jane Roberts) built up from mental and mathematical constructs. But so *also* are the technologies and technological products constructed on the basis of these sciences. These too are *idea constructions* - but *perceptible* ones, as opposed to the abstract mathematical constructions of science. In this sense Heisenberg was both right and wrong when he wrote, ignoring the primary reality of consciously *perceived* reality, i.e. the languages of *the senses* rather than mathematics, that "... modern physics has definitely decided in favour of Plato. In fact the smallest units of matter are not physical objects in the ordinary sense; they are forms, *ideas which can be expressed unambiguously only in mathematical language.*" [my italics]

We construe *perceptible* idea constructions as 'material' only because they can not only be seen, thought or imagined but also touched – tangibly felt and experienced in a tactile way. As for 'matter', this is an idea merely *abstracted* from our everyday perception of tangibly perceived tactile qualities such as weight and hardness. We may see what we *think of* as a 'pot' or 'kettle', can feel its hardness or weight, and handle it for our use – but we can *never* see, feel or handle the indeterminate substance called 'matter' that is *supposed* to have such things as weight and hardness as its 'properties'. Instead, this supposed material 'substance', like 'energy', is no more than an *idea* – not something like a pot or kettle that we can touch, handle and use for a specific purpose.

In fact we only see a pot or kettle *as* a pot or kettle, rather than a nameless perception, because in it we recognise a tactile potential for touching, feeling and handling it *for* such a purpose. Someone who knew nothing of modern technologies might recognise a chair as a chair, but certainly not see or recognise a computer or its keyboard *as* a computer or keyboard because in looking at or touching it they would not recognise its potential use. All they might recognise is something on the keyboard akin to whatever script or hieroglyphs they use – perhaps for religious purposes or with a sacred meaning. But one thing we cannot say is that ancient civilisations did not have their own complex artefacts and constructions. To many of these they attributed great power. And many of them were constructed in ways and to degrees of precision that would be impossible for us to reproduce – using even the most advanced construction technologies we have available today.

But the real point is this: what we see as the working technologies and instruments we have today are, like those of the past, mere tangible three-dimensional reflections of the ideas and idea constructions behind them. They do not in any way prove the greater technological superiority or efficacy of modern 'science'. And they are certainly no proof of this science having any greater *truth* than belief systems of the past. The fact that we can boil water in something we call an 'electric kettle' or cook food in a something we call a 'microwave' oven – rather than a simple pot – in no way proves the superior *truth* of our modern, 'scientific' belief system compared with belief systems of the past. In fact it says nothing about *truth* at all – but is only a reflection *of o*ur current belief system and its most widely worshipped religion – the religion of 'science'.

Finally, in what way can it be argued that modern technology 'works' better or more efficiently than technologies of the past when we consider the *price* we are now paying for that 'progress' and 'efficiency' – in the form of ecological devastation and the degradation of nature? Can a technology which ends up *destroying* precisely those natural elements and phenomena which are the very 'objects' of the science on which it is based be said to be more 'advanced', or to express a more 'advanced' understanding *of* nature?

As regards medical science and technology, if this 'works' so effectively, why is it that the statistics published in the Journal of the American Medical Association in the United States show that 'scientific' medical treatments, surgery and drugs are responsible for more deaths than heart-disease and cancer? Why is it that sufferers of cancer are more and not less likely to die as a result of medical treatment, and why is it that most major improvements in both social and individual health have come about through improved sanitation, living conditions and general quality of life – and not from the latest medical treatments or technologies? The established scientific or 'medical model' of health is a simplistic 'cause and cure' model which denies any dimension of life *meaning* to illness and its potentially healing value[1].

Meanwhile biological *psychiatry* has become an ever-more obvious 'medical model' of the way in which 'scientific' research and new diagnostic labels are used to 'scientifically' *construct* one new 'disorder' after another – turning 'science' into a mere ideological arm of the pharmaceutical industry.

Genetic 'science' is now playing an increasing role in modern 'scientific' medicine. Yet as Heidegger pointed out, the genetic 'explanation' of illness "… suffers from a deficit which is all too easily and therefore all too often overlooked. To be in a position to explain an illness genetically, we need first of all to explain what the illness in itself *is*. It may be that a true understanding of the essence of an illness…prohibits all causal-genetic explanation ... Those who wish to stick rigidly to genetic explanation, without first of all clarifying the essence of that which they wish to explain, can be compared to people who wish to reach a goal, without first of all bringing this goal in view. All explanation reaches only so far as the explication of that which is to be explained."

---

[1] See *The Illness is the Cure*, Peter Wilberg

Myth 12

Science does not need 'God' to explain the world by the so-called 'law of causality'.

Religion explains the world on the basis of God being it 'First Cause'.

It is a paradox that all major religions and theologies share with modern science what is perhaps the most common but least questioned belief of all – a belief in the principle or 'law' of causality. It makes no difference whether the 'First Cause' of the world is seen as a Supreme Being or a Big Bang, the belief is the same. It makes no difference either whether we speak of commonplace events or religious miracles being 'caused' by the action of some thing, person or being – the belief is the same. At the very foundation of both science and religions therefore, not only in their present forms but in all their past forms too, lies an idea that is taken as so obvious that it is never even questioned – namely the idea of *causality*.

The German word for 'cause' is *Ursache* – meaning 'original thing' (*Ur-sache*). Yet neither in physics, medicine – or life – is there any original 'thing' that is the 'cause' of all other things. In this context, the very idea of a 'First Cause' actually contradicts the law of causality itself – which denies there is anything that causes another thing but is itself free of causes. Nor does the notion of a First Cause in any way answer Heidegger's fundamental question of being – of why there *is* anything at all – *including* any putative 'First Cause' – rather than nothing.

Many reasons can be put forward for rejecting the principle of causality, whatever form it may take – not least as a basic scientific principle or 'law'? How so, one might ask? For if one billiard ball hits another, does it not *cause* it to move? Or if we press a light switch or 'on' button does this not 'cause' the light to go on or to activate whatever equipment we are dealing with? One major problem with the principle of causality is that action is essentially *interaction* – *mutual* or *reciprocal* action. Even when one billiard ball hits a second ball, the first ball does not 'cause' an alteration in the velocity and trajectory of the second. The velocity of *both* balls is immediately altered by their *interaction* – an interaction in which both balls compress and decompress *at the same time.*

The act of flipping a switch to turn a light on is not only an example of *interaction* – in this case with the switch itself. For the essence of this interaction is not that it 'causes' a light to go on but that it *permits* or *allows* further processes of interaction to follow and a further experience to unfold in awareness (that of a light going on). All this occurs within a larger *process* of action and experiencing that in no way *begins* with or is caused by the action and experience of flipping the switch – or even with the *experience* of oneself as the principal agent of the action and 'cause' of its 'effect'. For this experience is just that – one *experience* among others.

Perhaps we might even take a hint from the Bible here. God says 'LET there be light' – which could be paraphrased as saying 'Let the light be' – rather than 'causing' it to be.

'Effects' are supposed to follow 'causes' in time. Yet at each stage in any process of change, the *interactions* that form part of it are instantaneous. The supposed 'causes' and 'effects' are *instantaneous* reciprocal *interactions* that co-occur and cannot be separated in time. Seeing lightning and hearing thunder may appear to us as separable events in time, one 'causing' the other, but they are not essentially separable at all. Thunder is only seen as an event *separable* from and 'caused' by lightning since it is only heard after an interval of silence *in time*. But the thunderous shock wave created in the air by the lightning is an event initiated at the same time as lightning itself. Thunder and lightning are but two distinct and essentially *inseparable* sides of the same *singular* phenomenon – a 'thunderbolt'.

The concept of causality implies that any process of change is divisible into a linear, uni-directional chain of *separable* causes and effects. But process and change – 'becoming' – is essentially indivisible into separable parts. It is an indivisible and singular process, like the growth of a plant in the soil or of a foetus in the womb, one which cannot be reduced to a linear chain of *separable* causes and effects. No one would argue that the soil 'causes' a seed to grow or that a plant stem 'causes' flower buds to emerge and unfold from it. Instead, like all processes, organic processes are not reducible to chains of causes and effects.

The Greek word for cause (*aitia*) meant something closer to a 'reason' or 'explanation' for something rather than its 'cause' in a mechanistic sense. The German word for 'reason' is *ground*. Plants need a ground – soil – on which to grow, just as animals need ground to move or stand on. Yet though a *field* of soil is the *ground* upon which the trees, grass and flowers grow and animals move it is neither the 'cause' of their growth or movement nor a sufficient explanation (*aitia*) for it, but merely a *condition* for it.

All supposedly causal relations *assume* certain *conditions*. So for an electric spark to cause a fire in a room or house there must also be oxygen in it. The distinction between *conditions* and *causes* allows us to deconstruct the supposed 'law' of causality. For as soon as we recognise the conditions necessary for an apparently causal relationship to manifest, the relationship ceases to be causal in the strict sense that one thing *necessarily* follows another – independently of different conditions and contexts. Thus in the case of a fire supposedly 'caused' by a spark we could equally well assert that it was 'caused' by the presence of oxygen. This paradox can only be resolved by removing the notion of causality entirely and instead speaking solely of the *contexts* or *conditions* for the emergence or manifestation of any and all events and phenomena.

The whole notion of causality is based on several flawed assumptions. One is that action can be unidirectional or linear – thus causing an event, when in reality all action is a form of reciprocal or mutual interaction. Another assumption is that experienced events or occurrences cannot only be distinguished but also *separated* both from *one another* and also from the contextual *fields* of interrelatedness and underlying field states and conditions in which they emerge. Hence the example of thunder, which is only seen as an event *separable* from and 'caused' by lightning because the far slower speed of sound makes it appear that the thunder (an auditory experience) *followed* the lightning (a visual experience) after an interval *in time*. But the fact that auditory and visual experiences are distinct events does not mean they are separable. Nor does the fact that people may die from a lightning strike mean that their death can be said to have been the 'result' or 'effect' *caused* by the action of the lightning on their body. This implies that the bodies of those struck by lightning are passive inert objects of its action on them and that their death involved no physiological *interaction* with the lightning bolt. We know also that it requires certain atmospheric *field-conditions* for lightning to occur. We know also that even given these field conditions it is impossible to predict exactly when and where the lightning will occur.

No elaborate physical-scientific notion such as 'quantum entanglement' is needed to explain or prove *a-causal* connections or the reciprocal interrelatedness of all phenomena. Such notions are scientific mystifications of types of common experiences – like having a hunch that someone is about to call you before they do or at least before your phone rings.

In physics this is deemed impossible, since, given the limitation of the speed at which light or of any form of so-called 'energy' can travel, you cannot possibly know that someone is calling or has called you until the electromagnetic energy which is the medium of connection reaches your phone. Any awareness of someone calling you can therefore only come about after a *time interval* that is equal to or below the speed of light.

Yet physics, in principle, restricts reality as such to a hypothetical light cone spreading out in time and at a finite speed of light from an event E. It is because the *only* type of events that can occur in this cone are limited by the speed of light that they are conceived as 'causal' events or 'time-like' (Roger Jones).[2] Physical science ignores the entire dimension of reality *surrounding* the hypothetical light cone, a dimension in

---

[2] Jones, Roger *Physics as Metaphor* Abacus, 1983

which all events would have a purely 'space-like' character which lacks the fourth dimension of *time* central to both the idea of causality and compound scientific concept of 'space-time'). Causality is only possible because of an objective time difference between 'cause' and 'effect' ensured by a finite speed of light. What is called the speed of light is therefore effectively 'the speed of causality'.

"Because signals and other causal influences cannot travel faster than light (see special relativity and quantum entanglement), the light cone plays an essential role in defining the concept of causality: for a given event E." (Wikipedia)

Of course, the intimate relation between time and causality has long been recognised in both philosophy and science. This brings us to the crux of the whole question of causality – the nature of time. The idea of time as a line of point-like 'nows' is a fiction and also an implicitly *spatial* construct, as is the notion of events occurring 'in' time. But what if time really is a dimension of space – understood simply as a *co-presence* of experienced events rather than their temporal succession. Our lived subjective experience of time – which is our sole 'empirical' starting point for an understanding of time – itself points to this. For within the field of awareness that constitutes the 'present', both past and future are themselves *co-present* – like the co-presence of an experienced need for switching on a light ('past'), and the anticipation of the light coming on (future) in the very act of switching it on ('present').

The Awareness Principle understands awareness as the ground of all things – their common *field* of emergence – but not their 'cause'. And precisely because it is the ground of all things, awareness is also that which connects all things, like the intertwining or interconnected roots of plants and trees beneath the surface of the ground. Awareness, however, unlike what is called 'energy', is not constrained by any 'speed'. If we hold a particular person in awareness, the particular awareness we have of them (our way of seeing them, our thoughts and feelings about them and our intents towards them – like calling them by phone) communicates *instantaneously* to that person in a way that transcends the speed of light. Awareness is what feels things – and in feeling them also touches them. In the same way that flowing air or wind touches our skin, so is awareness the very medium by which we feel and touch the souls of others. Indeed what we call 'soul' is nothing other than this feeling nature and activity of awareness itself.

An *awareness* of the 'past' and anticipation of the 'future' that form part of the 'present' – as a space of co-presence – does not in itself contain any element of causal succession. Put simply: the awareness of time as a succession of moments and events is not *itself* anything successive or temporal. Instead, as philosopher Edmund Husserl had the perspicuity to see, there is a fundamental correspondence between this experience of time and the experience of music and speech – in which any 'past' word or tone continues to *resound* in the present, whilst at the same time being a prelude to or anticipation of the next word or tone. A stretch of speech, like a musical melody, may appear to manifest in successive words or tones but what manifests is a patterned field of words or tones which are essentially *co-present* – whether as actual or potential words or tones, in the stretch of speech or melody *as a whole*. One tone in a melody or one word in a stretch of speech does not *cause* the next to appear, and nor is it *caused* by a preceding word or tone. Thus when we begin to speak, we neither know with what word our sentence will end nor does anything we have said determine or cause those final words. The stretch of speech is a *singular creative process* and event – no element of which can be said to cause another.

As in speech and music, so also in all things – all dimensions of our lived experience. What is experienced is not a causal sequence but a *pattern of acausal interrelatedness* –whether of tones, speech, or any type of lived and experienced events or phenomena. Thus to regard causal connections as the *rule* and reduce acausal connections to an *exception* in the form of rare events of "synchronicity", as Jung did, is not only wrong – it is contradicted by our every experience of speech and music.

Myth 13

Science has generated an effective, rational and 'evidence-based' approach to medicine.

Religion offers only irrational approaches to medicine lacking any evidence.

"The idea of one basis for science and another for life is, from the very outset, a lie."

Karl Marx

"Modern medical 'science' adopts an almost wholly causalistic approach to illness. In doing so however, it artificially separates the life of the *human being* from the life of the *human body*, thus denying from the outset, any *meaning* to illness – and neither seeing nor seeking an understanding of the social and individual *life conditions and contexts* in which particular symptoms or illnesses emerge, and which endow them *with* meaning."

"Disease occurs ... not in the body, but in life."

J. Good Byron

"That illnesses have meaning – this is the insight that natural-scientific medicine has fundamentally impeded."

Viktor von Weizsäcker

Whereas traditional religion recognised *meaning* in illness, even if only in the simplistic and moralistic form of 'karma' or punishment for sin, biological medicine simply and mechanistically reduces the meaning of illness to its supposed biological 'causes'.

The body is reduced by modern medicine to a living biological *machine* – rather than being understood as a living biological *language* of the human being – its fleshly text. The result is that no consideration at all is given to what the body may be seeking to *say* through the language of illness, or to the way in which an illness may give biological expression to the real life conflicts and problems of the patient – and to the felt *dis-ease* experienced along with them.

Hence, as Dr. David Zigmond writes: "There is no need to explore or amplify the experience", which is seen "only as the reflection of a disturbed underlying mechanism" whose physical manifestation only needs to be medicated or engineered away.

The 'cause and cure' model of medicine (shared by mainstream medicine and most forms of 'alternative' medicine alike) is based instead on a diagnostic witch-hunt aimed at diagnosing a medically labelled disease that is 'causing' the patient's symptoms. One of the main reasons patients go to doctors is to seek such a diagnosis – fear it though they may.

As Michael Balint M.D. wrote in his classic work 'The Doctor, His Patient and the Illness':

"For the patient, illness is always an uncanny experience. He feels something has gone wrong with him, something that might, or certainly will do him harm unless dealt with

properly swiftly. What 'it' is, is difficult to know. Often 'it' becomes identical with its name, and for the patient the function of the diagnosis is to supply the name by which this uncanny, malevolent and frightening something can be called, thought of, and perhaps dealt with ... In other words, being ill is still often thought of, and is certainly felt as meaning being possessed by some evil, and the belief is rampant, not only among patients, that the devil can be driven out only if his name is known."

In other words, just as in many cultures illness used to be thought of as 'caused' by a malevolent spirit, one which needed to be exorcised by a witchdoctor or shaman, so today the cause is sought through the diagnosis of a malign physiological 'disease' which must be subjected to medical or surgical exorcism.

The Wikipedia definition of 'diagnosis' is "the identification of the *nature and cause* of a certain phenomenon". But to identify the *nature* of a phenomenon and to identify its *cause* are two quite distinct things. In much everyday medical practice, diagnosis consists purely in reducing the *nature* of the patient's symptoms to an accepted diagnostic label.

Yet this act of naming or labelling the patient's symptoms is *neither* an identification of their cause *nor* a broader or deeper *explanation* of them. Instead it merely *substitutes* for one of two things – *either* a purely causal explanation of the illness that is named *or* a meaning-based explanation – one which recognises the illness itself as a *symptom* of problems in the patient's life. Medical psychiatry, for example, whilst recognising, for example, that the term 'depression' is a mere *diagnostic label* for a set of *symptoms* – at the same time treats it as if it were some 'thing in itself' – a disease entity or 'disorder' called 'depression' that is the *cause* of those symptoms and is in need of exorcism through psychiatric medications.

People might have all sorts of good and commonly recognised *life reasons* for feeling 'depressed' – for example unemployment, poverty, relationship problems, bereavement etc. – 'scientific' psychiatry seeks to reduce these understandable life *reasons* to purely physiological *causes*. And instead of seeking meaningful life *explanation*s or *reasons* for why people might feel depressed, it treats 'depression' – like *all* illnesses – as some independent 'disease entity' or 'thing in itself' present in or 'possessing' the patient's body and mind – and then in turn seeks the 'cause' of this 'thing' or 'entity' in some other thing – for example in a supposed 'deficit' of certain neurotransmitters in their brain and nervous system.

Here psychiatry presents us with a perfect model of the way in which scientific medicine is not in the least bit 'evidence based' – since no evidence has ever been found of a such a pre-existing deficit or 'chemical imbalance' in a person diagnosed with depression. On the other hand, there is ample evidence of psychiatric medications generating changes in brain chemistry and functioning in a way which actually worsens the patient's condition or even leads to death. A clear example of this is the use of SSRI type 'antidepressants', prescribed on a massive scale even though the 'scientific research' has frequently shown them to have little or no significant effect compared with a placebo. And one causally unpredicted and unpredictable 'effect' of their use is in fact suicidal thoughts – and in many cases actual suicide. It took a long time for the pharma corporations to admit this – and even longer to actually warn in their information leaflets that taking their 'antidepressants', far from preventing suicide in extreme cases, may lead to suicidal ideation if not actual suicide. Indeed it is likely that these medications are behind many horrific incidents of school shootings and massacres by lone perpetrators.

Far from being 'rational' then, medical science reduces 'reasons' or 'explanations' (the real meaning of the Greek word for 'cause' (*aitia*) to mere causes in the *mechanistic* sense.

Reasons for thinking, feeling or acting in a certain way can be freely *questioned* by rational reflection – by *reasoning*. Reasons and reasoning are thus the basis of both freedom of thought and freedom of action – free will. The search for 'causes' on the other hand, implies a type of physical or biological determinism, which rules out both free will and free thinking. *In reducing reasons to causes science throws both rationality and free will out of its world view.*

Furthermore, the 'rationality' of scientific thinking as such collapses in on itself as soon as we accept the current 'scientific' belief that 'rational' thinking as such is merely the autonomous, unwilled biological activity of some bodily 'thing' – *the brain* – rather than a free and independent activity of *mind*. For if thinking *is* merely an autonomous activity of the brain, then how and by what independent 'rational' criteria can its 'rationality' be judged? Medical science then, does not express the heights of 'rational' thinking, but is instead its very opposite – an irrational, self-contradictory worldview parading itself as the very paradigm of rationality.

Yet by far the most damning argument *against* both the rationality and effectiveness of medical 'science' is that – from *its own evidence*, and as reported in its own *leading journals* and from its *own studies* – modern medical treatment has itself become, in its own terms one of the leading *causes* of illness and even death, ahead even of cancer and heart disease!

The question of medical *iatrogenesis* – the genesis of an illness through a physician or healer (Greek *iatros*) is a highly significant one, also since it sheds further light on the so-called 'law' of causality. For one must not forget that in speaking of 'laws' of nature – in particular a 'law' of causality, one is imposing a human *social* concept – the rule of 'law' – onto nature, the human body and human experiencing in general. Closely connected with 'law' in the social sense however, are also social ideas of order and stability and *morality* on the one hand, and of *guilt and punishment* on the other. One reason why – as Ivan Illich noted long ago – *iatrogenic* illness and death has reached *epidemic* proportions (pandemic would now be a more fitting word) is that the so-called 'law' of causality is not a law of nature but a law that is actively consented to or *enforced* on the patient – just as if it *were* a 'law' in the *social* sense.

Medical enforcement of 'the law' constitutes a type of *violation* of the body comparable to the punishment of a *crime* committed by the human body. In the worst case, it amounts to a type of long term prison sentence for the patient or even a form of capital punishment – taking the form of acute, chronic or even fatal 'side-effects'.

It is not just that medical treatments enforce this 'law' of causality in the name of 'science'. In many cases, social and criminal law is itself applied to violently enforce medication or medical treatment upon patients – for example by imposing penalties on parents who do not have their children vaccinated (or even taking them away) or by forcing some types of 'mental patient' to take brain-toxic medications – *using* both the force of the law but even physical force. As a result, any patient who doubts, questions or refuses a standard form of prescribed testing or treatment is spoken of as 'uncompliant' – in the same way that someone who challenges or defies a legal judgement or process is seen as 'in contempt' of court. The difference is that medical professionals act as both judge, juror and enforcer of the 'penalty', that it is the patient's *body* rather than the person that is seen as the chief suspect or perpetrator of the 'crime' – the crime of generating illness – and that it is the human body that is impersonally 'sentenced' and 'punished' by prescription or surgery.

This all reminds one less of 'rationality' and 'science' as most people understand it than of a form of religious inquisition and persecution based on paranoia – and in particular on a paranoid relation to the human body justified in the name of medical science – which all-too often suspects the body of trying to *murder* the patient through one disease or another – rather than *serving* the patient as a form of unconscious self-expression.

Myth 14

Science does not persecute 'heretics'.

Religion does.

Both Judaeo-Christianity and Islam are infamous for their persecution of religious heresy and heretics – not least the notorious attack by The Church on Galileo. Yet today, anyone who questions for example, the supposed 'scientific' fact that smoking is a major 'cause' of cancer would be regarded as no less *heretical* in the face of 'The Science' than a Galileo was in the face of 'The Church'.

Yet whereas accusations of religious heresy could in the past be challenged in religious courts, anyone seeking to legally defend their right to smoke in public places would today have no right to question in court the *entire framework and foundation* of 'The Science' that denies that right. Nor would they be given legal opportunities today to offer rational arguments showing that anti-smoking propaganda *is itself responsible* for more cancer-related deaths than smoking itself – working as it does like a damagingly negative counterpart of the *placebo* effect on which the effectiveness of so much 'scientific' medication rests. That modern medical treatments for disease are, as has been pointed out earlier, the 3rd major cause of death or that psychiatric medications aimed at 'treating' anxiety and psychosis are themselves responsible for a *veritable plague of psychoses and suicides* – these are some of the 'facts' that sit uncomfortably with today's unquestioned faith in the authority of Science, a faith as difficult and 'heretical' to question today as the dogmas and authority of The Church were in the past. 'Scientific' medicine *is just one example among many* of how the repression of scientific 'heresy' does not go without its own human consequences – in this case the persecution and suffering of countless people tricked or forced by the supposed 'scientific' authority of doctors into taking life-threatening, addictive, psychosis- or suicide-inducing prescription drugs.

Scientists themselves however are far from immune to persecution. Quite the opposite – hardly a single major new idea in science has not been *preceded and delayed* by the most rabid attacks – often tantamount to accusations of heresy – not just on the new concepts or theories themselves, but against the persons who originated them. Isaac Asimov distinguished between two types of scientific heretic:

"Endoheretics are appropriately credentialed scientists. If the person is outside the scientific community or at least outside of his specialty, he is an exoheretic. If a person is an endoheretic, he will be considered as eccentric and incompetent, whereas if the person is an exoheretic, he will be regarded as a crackpot, charlatan, or fraud."

A recent and still on-going example of the scientific persecution and 'excommunication' of endoheretics is the attack on the biologist Rupert Sheldrake – author of a second book with the same title as this one: *The Science Delusion*. The radically new yet well-argued theory advanced in his first book *A New Science of Life* received the following response from the editor of the British Journal of Nature, Sir John Maddox: "This infuriating tract…is the best candidate for burning there has been for many years."

It cannot be denied that institutionalised religions often *deliberately seek* to restrict freedom of thought – confining it to the lexicon of their own officially authorized 'canons' of scripture, and the specific language and symbolism they employ. Yet the sciences too, have not only generated a whole range of new, *no less thought-confining* jargons and terminologies of their own, but have gone even further – abolishing all *awareness* of the way in which these terminologies can, in and of themselves, restrict freedom of thought by confining it in the framework of their own unquestioned terms and lexicons. In many ways the scientific worldview is one that is held even more tightly in the grip of its own unquestioned terminologies than religious theologies – which have a long and venerable history of exploring and re-interpreting the *meaning* of their own, most sacred words, symbols and scriptures.

Myth 15

Science has to do with facts alone.

Religion has to do with values.

To so neatly compartmentalise the respective realms of science and religion in terms of a simplistic dualism of experimentally observed 'facts' and ethical 'values' is misleading. It implies that our 'scientific' understanding of relations *between* things and between people is something entirely 'value neutral', having nothing to do with what is the very essence of 'ethics' – namely our relation *to* things and *to* people. It forgets that the way we understand the complex relations between things and between beings is shaped, from the beginning, by the nature of our relation *to* them.

"The relation that constitutes knowing is one in which we ourselves are related and in which this relation vibrates through our basic posture."

"… it seems necessary to characterise our entirely different method as *specifically engaging in our relationship* to what we encounter…"

"In a sense, what is characteristic of phenomenology is the will not to resist this engaging-oneself."

Martin Heidegger

If we grant all our awareness to contemplating and fully taking in a landscape, animal or person, our 'observation' of that landscape, animal or person, reveals its truth or reality to us in a quite different way to how it would do if instead we merely set about digging up or mining the land, conducting experiments on animals, or wiring up the bodies and brains of human beings to machines.

The scientific worldview and scientific experimentation and observation is not in any way value-neutral because it expresses a specific *relation* to the world – what Martin Buber called an 'I-It' relation in contrast to an 'I-You' relation. As Marx saw, it belongs to the very nature of capitalism to turn all human values into commodities, and in doing so to reduce all authentic relations between beings – which have the character of an 'I-You' relation – to a relation between things or commodities – an 'I-It' or even 'It-It' relation.

Thus all relations between human beings and the world are reduced to a relationship between the human brain (a mere thing or 'It') and a world of things. Consequently also, relations between human beings are effectively reduced to relationships between their brains or genes. The legal profession is already aware of the 'ethical' implications of this idea, which would logically imply for example, that criminal acts are not a result of the perversion of all human relations into an 'I-It' relation – human beings treating each other as mere things or objects, motivated by the desire to accumulate things and objects. No, for scientifically understood there is no 'I' or 'being' in the first place – only a brain with the delusion of an autonomous, free-willed self or 'I'.

Not only is the scientific worldview not value neutral. In its relation *to* the world – a relation determined by technology – it ends up giving free ethical reign to the most ruthless and 'unethical' forms of experimentation, exploitation and ultimately destruction. That it may do so in the name of 'knowledge' and not just for commercial profit should not delude us. For the *type* of knowledge gained is narrow in the extreme – limited precisely by its prime purpose – the application of technology in the pursuit of profit. Does all this mean we should abandon the lifestyle that modern technology with its televisions, mobile phones and computers offers us? Surely such technology is practical proof, not of the delusory nature of science but of its truth and enormous value?

This brings us back again to the last-ditch defence of the 'Science Delusion' – the 'argument from technology' that claims that its ability to create effective and practical technical appliances is evidence of the truth of science. Yet is it? Our common sense understanding of everyday appliances such as televisions and computers tells us that they are designed on the basis of scientific knowledge, then built in dedicated factories, bit-by-bit, so that they can finally be shipped to us and become part of our lives, life-world and 'lifestyle'.

This common sense view applies not just to the latest but to the very earliest forms of modern industrial technology and its products – everything from the steam engine to electricity generation, light bulb, radios and modern automobiles. How is it then that modern physics *itself* tells us that this common sense view is simply *not scientifically true*? For according to quantum physicists such as Hawking, whilst it may seem that your television or computer came from a factory in China, in reality its every atom and particle is constantly manifesting from an invisible but all-pervasive quantum 'vacuum'.

In other words, the mobile phone you pick up or the television or computer screen you look at today is *not* the one built in a factory – or even the one you picked up or perceived a minute or even a nanosecond ago! For matter – all matter – is constantly emerging from and disappearing back into a quantum vacuum. What exactly this quantum 'field' or 'vacuum' *is* no physicists can say. Yet what they *are* saying could have and has been said in a quite different way and from a quite different perspective. It was said by those ancient sages, who declared that every aspect of our experienced world – and everything in it – is constantly and continuously manifesting from a vast and infinite field of *consciousness.*

The mystifying mathematical complexities of quantum physics are the last attempt to both deny and mystify this simplest and yet most primordial truth of all – the truth that it is no mysterious 'quantum void' but rather *consciousness* itself which is the *sole reality* behind and within all things – and the source of them all. Not 'my' consciousness or 'yours' but consciousness *as such*, understood as an infinite, all-pervasive field of pure awareness, one latent with infinite *potentialities* of expression that are constantly manifesting as every existing thing we experience – from a rock to a laptop. Hence a saying of the great 10th century Indian sage Abhinavagupta: **"The being of all things that are recognised in awareness in turn depends on awareness"** – an understanding reaffirmed by the physicist Max Planck in the 20th century: **"Everything that we talk about, everything that we regard as existing, presupposes consciousness."**

Postscript

The 'Science Delusion' is more than just a delusion. It is the dictatorship, not of an individual, but of an irrationalist and self-contradictory worldview more dangerous than the most fundamentalist, dogmatic and totalitarian forms of institutionalised religion or ideology. Institutionalised religion in the form of 'The Church' once openly and almost totally dominated the culture of Europe, as fundamentalist Islam now openly seeks its own form of global ideological domination. Yet 'The New Church of Science' (not the so-called 'Church of Scientology', which is but an ugly mirror image of scientific ideology itself) is far more dangerous than any self-professed church or religious cult. That is because its dogmatic, fundamentalist, irrationalist, destructive and totalitarian nature remains almost *wholly invisible* – not only to its lay believers but even to its most fervent high priests.

At the heart of 'The Church' that is now duly called '*The Science*' is the urge to seek 'explanations' and 'causes' for things – rather than *exploring* and directly *experiencing* more deeply what they essentially *are* and *mean*. Taken to its logical conclusion, science would seek to 'explain' words themselves as 'effects' rather than *expressions* of meaning – with meanings seen as their quasi-deterministic 'cause'. Given its confusion of causal explanations with reasons and meanings it is no wonder that science cannot satisfy people's search for a rational understanding of the 'meaning of life' – what Viktor Frankl called 'the Will to Meaning' at the heart of our being, and of religious experience. True 'science' – true *knowledge* – can neither arise by reducing the *subjective reality* of our lived experience to explanatory *causes* nor by seeking to counter orthodox 'scientific' explanations of nature (evolution for example) with counter-explanations drawn from religious myths.

Both ways reflect 'The Science Delusion' – the confusion of *reasons* with deterministic *causes*, and of meaningful subjective experiences of reality with 'objective' explanations. Yet what if people could *escape* from this delusion? What if they knew that, being *a part of* the entire universe, they could each explore the entire universe *from within themselves* – directly, experientially, and *without the aid of any scientific instruments or equations*? This is no mere hypothetical question. For there have always been and still are individuals who *know* this – from *direct experience*. Indeed whole civilizations have been built around this type of direct experiential or 'phenomenological' knowledge. And as Heidegger emphasised, it is such primordial *knowledge* (German *Wissen*) that belongs to the very essence of *science* as *Wissen-schaft*. Yet what the 'Science Delusion', as I have described it here, has most effectively succeeded in concealing is the existence of wholly *different* understandings of and approaches to 'science' to the modern one, which has come (if only in the last few centuries) to be taken as definitive, and exclusive of all others. Yet other models of science have survived and evolved from the ancient past to this very day. They include not only 'phenomenological science', but also what has been termed 'sacred science', 'yogic science', 'spiritual science', 'dialectical science', 'hermeneutic science', 'integral science', 'qualitative science' and 'subjective science'. The essential principles and primary methodologies of *direct experiential research and experimentation* that could together constitute a newer and truer science of the *future* is the subject of my book: *The Qualia Revolution - from Quantum Physics to Cosmic Qualia Science*

.

Appendix 1

A Science Teacher in Big Trouble

Many teachers of religion are used to being asked uncomfortable questions to which they can come up with no answers satisfactory for their students or even logically consistent in any way. The same applies to teachers of 'science' – but unfortunately far more rarely. Example: extract from an educational site on the concept of 'energy' for children and science teachers:

*Energy is defined as: "**the ability to do work.**" We use energy to do work. Energy lights our cities. Energy powers our vehicles, trains, planes and rockets. Energy warms our homes, cooks our food, plays our music, gives us pictures on television. Energy powers machinery in factories and tractors on a farm. Energy from the sun gives us light during the day. It dries our clothes when they're hanging outside on a clothes line. It helps plants grow. Energy stored in plants is eaten by animals, giving them energy. And predator animals eat their prey, which gives the predator animal energy. Everything we do is connected to energy in one form or another.*

*When we eat, our bodies transform the energy stored in the food into energy to do work. When we run or walk, we "burn" food energy in our bodies. When we think or read or write, we are also doing work. Many times it's really **hard** work! Cars, planes, light bulbs, boats and machinery also transform energy into work. Work means moving something, lifting something,* *warming something, lighting something. All these are a few of the various types of work.*

Anyone see any problem with these assertions and this account of 'energy'? A philosopher would certainly see not just one but many problems. Here are just a few:

The authors do not say by *whom, when or for what reason* energy 'is defined' as 'the ability to do work'.

If what is called 'energy' really is this *"ability to do work"*, then to say that '*we use energy to do work*' is simply to say that we use 'the ability to do work' to ……. do work! What an amazing scientific revelation!

Cars, planes, light bulbs, boats and machinery also transform energy into work. What exactly it means to 'transform' an 'ability to do work' (energy) 'into work' is not explained.

It is not explained how energy, as this *'ability to do work'* is what 'lights our cities', 'powers our vehicles' etc. – or how this *'ability to do work'* can be 'stored in plants', 'eaten by animals', in this way *'giving them energy'*.

These types of definition and expression are clearly circular and tautological. They simply say that an 'ability to work' can, in different ways, result in 'an ability to do work!

Scientists used to and still do accuse philosophers of writing scientific nonsense. The truth is the other way round. It is not the philosophers who are scientifically 'illiterate'. It is the scientists who are *philosophically* illiterate – who write *philosophical* nonsense – full of tautologies, circular arguments or contradictions.

But not all science students are stupid. Some ask serious questions! Below is a question posed by a science student regarding the standard idea, still taught in all schools, that electrical 'current' is a 'flow' of 'electrons' in a 'conductor':

We know that electrons are free to move about in a conductor...they have a drift velocity of 1cm/s, yet when we see any conductor (antenna for eg.), the electron actually does not move along the whole length of the conductor, it just vibrates about its mean position and its energy moves ahead. How is it that the energy the electron produces moves ahead of itself? Secondly, in an AC circuit, the voltage changes its polarity. Then how does current flow in its circuit? If I assume that the electron moves, then the moment the current reverses its polarity, the electron should move in the reverse direction, ie a step forward and a step backward. How does it move at all? If I assume that the electron does not move and the energy it produces moves, then also, how does it move? How do we actually get any current?

Here is the first part of the supposed 'answer' from a physicist':

"Fun questions! Conductors have many, many mobile electrons. For many metals, it is about one electron per atom which is free to move. These electrons have rather large velocities, due to the fact that they fill up energy levels just as the electrons in atoms fill up available energy levels. When an electric field is applied, they are mobile and quickly move (average net motion, on top of their random motion) to cancel out the field, and so a good low-frequency approximation is that electric fields are always zero inside of conductors."

In what way is this an answer to the student's question? In what way does it even make either grammatical, logical or 'scientific' sense to say that free electrons have *"rather large velocities due to the fact that they fill up energy levels just as the electrons in atoms fill up available energy levels."* For example, it is not at all clear from this sentence what the difference is between a "single electron per atom" filling up an electron 'hole' at a certain "energy level" in a nearby ionised atom and saying that such electrons "fill up available energy levels" per se?

The 'answer', part 2:

"As you say, when a conductor carries a current, the electrons have a net drift velocity which is often quite small. The actual drift velocity depends a lot on the geometry of the conductor, the amount of current flowing, and the density of mobile charge carriers (the drift velocity is proportional to the current, and inversely proportional to the cross-sectional area and the density of mobile charge carriers)."

This part of the answer refers to "the amount of current flowing" but not the student's question about the exact nature of this supposed 'flow' of 'current'? Note: it is also a questionable use of language to refer to a 'current' (i.e. a flow of some sort) as something which is itself 'flowing'. The answer continues:

"As you correctly say, in an AC circuit (with frequencies of 60 Hz here or 50 Hz where you are, or at radio frequencies), the electrons don't drift very far. But what happens is that a large number of electrons all collectively shift their positions together. When you apply an electric field to a conductor, each

electron only has to move a little bit, but all of them move together, and so the net current can be quite high."

This part of the answer is an attempt to trick the student. What the physicist is really saying is that there is no free flow of 'free electrons' in a conductor outside the atoms in it, but only a flow from one atom to another. He goes on to say:

"Signals propagate along wires at very high speeds. If a wire is perfectly conducting, then the speed of a signal propagating along depends on the insulating material around the wire. This is because the energy transfer is actually in the electric and magnetic fields. Poynting's vector is E cross B, and is proportional to the energy flow per unit area per unit time, and since the electric field vanishes inside a conductor, no energy flows inside a conductor (!), just outside, in the immediate vicinity. The speed of propagation of signals then depends on the dielectric properties of the insulation, and typically is about 70% of the speed of light. The electrons just flow in the conductor to satisfy the conditions of the electric and magnetic fields obeying Maxwell's equations on the surface of the conductor."

At last the physicist admits two things not taught to students of electricity, namely that 1. 'energy transfer' (his new term for 'current') does not actually occur at all 'inside a conductor' (!) but outside it, and 2. the very idea of electrons 'flowing' as a 'current' in a conductor is only needed for the purpose of obeying Maxwell's equations. In other words it is the mathematical theory – *and not any empirical reality*, that determines the 'scientific explanation' of 'electrical currents'. Finally we are told by the physicist that:

"In reality, all electrons are indistinguishable (?) It is not a fair question to ask about where a single electron goes as it does not retain its identity separate from the other electrons. But the classical picture is sufficient to explain the answers to these questions. One question it does not explain is why the electrons in metals are so mobile, and why they don't bump into the atoms more, and quantum mechanics is needed for that one."

The physicist now complains that the question is 'unfair'. This comes from his recognition that in quantum mechanics (in contrast to what he calls the 'classical picture') an electron cannot even be said to have a clearly identifiable 'position' at all, but exists as a probability field or 'cloud' of positions. The physicist cannot himself reconcile classical models of the electron with quantum-mechanical models of where an electron is – or even *what* it is! So in attempting to answer the student's question about electrons and electron currents he effectively admits that he truly doesn't know what, in essence, he is actually talking about.

Thus in his attempt to 'explain' electron flow – what we think of as a commonplace form and example of 'energy' flow – the physicist has already to *use* the term 'energy' in a way that remains wholly unquestioned, undefined and unexplicated. This is an example of how scientific language consistently avoids the central philosophical challenge that Heidegger raised when he said that all *explanation* can only reach so far as the *explication* of what it is it seeks to explain. The result of this avoidance on the part of scientists is a type of linguistic mystification of the sort of that is evident in the above-quoted 'answers' to a student's question.

Nor do the answers begin to answer even more fundamental questions of the sort raised by physicist Dr. Roger S. Jones: **"How, for example, does the electric field of an electron affect the electron itself? Why doesn't the electron explode under the action of its own repulsive forces? If an electron is made up of some kind of distributed negative electric charge, why doesn't the mutual repulsion of all this concentrated negative charge force the electron to fly apart, just as two electrons that are brought together and released will fly apart? Is the electron immune to its own force? How is this possible? The laws of physics imply that all electric charge is susceptible to the electric field. Is there some stronger force that holds the electron together? But what is the nature of this force? Wouldn't this new force also be generated by some elementary particle at its source, just as the electron is the source of the electric field? And what would keep this new particle from exploding or collapsing under its own influence? Or are we to introduce a sequence of stronger and stronger forces ad infinitum, each successive force explaining its predecessor? Perhaps we can get around the whole problem by assuming that an electron is just a point with no finite size or spatial extension. But the electron has a finite mass and electric charge. It would then have an infinite density since the mass and charge would occupy zero volume. And how can a physical entity be a point? Matter in physics always takes up space. If a point electron were assumed to exist, would it be subject to** physical laws different from those that govern the external behaviour of electrons?"

Jones concludes:

"We have no way of visualizing how an unpicturable electron can possess a mass and a charge or how it can be present in space. We use such terms by analogy with our classical Newtonian models of matter, for which we have no other pictures to use. We are left with a theory that provides us with no ultimate unit of matter and no way of even picturing what we mean by matter. We only have the mathematical laws of quantum theory, with a prescription for getting numbers from them. And these numbers will correspond quite accurately, for the most part, with certain macroscopic measurements made in the laboratory. But exactly what it is we are ultimately measuring and how we are to picture and conceive of it is very difficult to say. So much for substance. Could Aristotle have foreseen this, he might well have thrown out of the Academy the entire subject matter."

Roger S. Jones *Physics as Metaphor*

Appendix 2

On 'Mind' and 'Matter': revisiting George Berkeley

It is high time for a philosopher to once again do what was last done by the great 18th century thinker George Berkeley. This is to deconstruct the very notions of mind 'and' matter, to recognise that 'matter' is itself an empty construct *of* the mind; and that a true and pure 'empiricist' – one who believes in the evidence of our sensory experience alone – is bound to conclude that there is no evidence whatsoever in that experience that behind the manifold sensory qualities of things, all of which are only ever experienced subjectively or 'in the mind', lies some objective but invisible 'substance' called 'matter'.

To be sure, we regularly experience things as hard or 'solid'. But this experience in no way supports the hypothesis that hardness and solidity are 'properties' of some solid material substance, of 'hard' or 'solid' matter. The same applies not only to all the supposedly 'secondary' qualities of matter – such as its warmth, colour, sound, smell and taste etc but also to what were seen as its 'primary qualities' – for example extension, size, distance etc.

The idea that modern electron microscopes can 'see' atoms of matter is absurd. Microscopes themselves 'see' nothing – only perceiving minds or consciousnesses such as human beings do that. But anything that *we* see with the help of an electron microscope – or any technical instrument of observation – is but a visual image or perception no different in essence from any other, i.e. offering no more evidence than any other that behind this perception is an invisible substance of the sort that is called 'matter'. Indeed the very fact that atoms appear enormously larger than they are supposed to be through an electron microscope is evidence that size itself is a relative quality, and therefore cannot, as Berkeley already argued, be seen as a fixed property of material substance, even if conceived as made up of atoms and particles.

Berkeley's 'immaterialism' may seem outlandish and contrary to common sense today, but in his own time it was certainly not. Ordinary people took it for granted that everything we perceive around us in the world was a phenomenal appearance or manifestation of God – a divine mind or consciousness, i.e. *not* the expression of other invisible or 'occult' entities such as intangible matter, gravity and other 'forces' or 'energies' soon to be invented in the minds of scientists (or 'natural philosophers' as they were still called) and also not the effect of objects on our sense organs and brain.

This last notion was first deconstructed by Berkeley in the following short section from that most wonderfully clear, lucid and elegantly written work of his: *Three Dialogues Between Hylas and Philonous* - one which I recommend a full reading of for anyone unconvinced by my short summary of its principal thesis – namely that direct sensory experience can never and in no circumstances offer any empirical evidence for the existence of matter, which is an empty construct of 'mind'.

Note that in his *Dialogues* Berkeley uses the term 'ideas' principally to refer to sensations or perceptions (a usage in resonance with the root meaning of the word 'idea' in the Greek verb ἰδεῖν - meaning to see or perceive, and the Greek word ἰδέα - which meant principally a perceived sensory quality, shape or form).

Hylas: It is supposed that the mind resides in some part of the brain, from which the nerves originate, spreading out from there to all parts of the body; that outer objects act in different ways on the sense-organs, starting up certain vibrations in the nerves; that the nerves pass these vibrations along to the brain (where the mind is located); and that the mind is variously affected with ideas [sense impressions] according to the various impressions or traces the vibrations make in the brain.

Philonous: And call you this an explanation of how we are affected with ideas?

Hylas: Why not, Philonous? Have you any objection to it?

Philonous: I need to know first whether I have rightly understood your 'modern' hypothesis. According to it, certain traces in the brain are the causes or occasions of our ideas. Tell me, please, do you mean by 'the brain' a sensible thing?

Hylas: What else do you think I could possibly mean?

Philonous: Sensible things are all immediately perceivable; and things that are immediately perceivable are ideas; and these exist only in the mind. This much, if I am not mistaken, you have long since agreed to.

Hylas: I don't deny it.

Philonous: So the brain that you speak of, being a sensible thing, exists only in the mind! I would like to know whether you think it reasonable to suppose that one idea or thing existing in

the mind occasions all the other ideas. And if you do think this,
how do you account for the origin of that primary idea or
'brain' itself?

I need not repeat here all the countless other arguments by which, in his *Dialogues*, Berkeley so elegantly and logically argues the case for immaterialism. What I can and will seek to do is to extend Berkeley's arguments not just to the classical scientific concept of matter – which, modern physics, in the form of quantum mechanics has done much to undo – but also to the modern scientific concept of 'energy' – one which has largely replaced the classical concept of matter. Yet even here, the impeccable logic of *Philonous* (a pseudonym for Berkeley himself) in his dialogues with Hylas (a stand-in for the philosopher John Locke) goes a long way in deconstructing the concept of 'energy' too.

To begin with, it can be helpful to turn our attention to the experience of hearing. A baby or 'infant' (from *in-fans,* meaning someone without speech or language) does not and cannot hear the sound of, say, 'a car passing by on the street'). Not only is a car something principally seen and recognised by its visual form, it is also and principally an adult's mental *idea* of and *word* for something seen – one that would not be shared by anyone who had never known or seen cars before. To go yet further and say that a car is also no objective material 'thing' of any sort may appear outlandish. And yet the actual experience of entering and seating oneself in 'a car', starting up the engine, going into gear, twisting the steering wheel and then driving along a road, is, in essence nothing but a series and combination of *subjective sensory experiences* – visual, auditory, tactile and kinaesthetic. The car only is 'a car' by virtue of the specific sequences and combinations of different types of sensory experiences associated with it.

As for how we come to hear the sound of a car – or any sound – Berkeley quickly and easily does away with the idea that hearing has to do with the effect of vibrations of molecules in the air affecting the eardrum, and through it, leading to an experience of sound 'in the brain'. For a vibration belongs to the realm of tactile sensation and not to hearing or auditory sensation. Therefore, as Berkeley argues, it does not explain how we hear *sounds*.

To also claim – as today's fashionable 'brain science' does – that all sensory experiences and perceptions, even our visual perceptions of objects, are essentially created BY the brain in response to external stimuli (photons or electromagnetic 'waves') is a notion loaded with paradox. For according to brain science itself, all supposedly material objects of vision are really just phantasms or hallucinations created by the brain as a result of processing what is loosely called sensory 'information'? But how could mere subjective phantasms or hallucinations of the brain be in any way capable of doing what the 'sciences' of both optics and neurophysiology assume them to be doing – reflecting 'light' which is then focussed by and impinges on the retina, thus affecting the brain via electromagnetic nerve signals and causing it to project a hallucinatory image of supposed 'objects' that are 'out there' in space? And is all that we are really doing when we find *meaning* in a great work of art just 'processing' something called sensory 'information' (a term that is merely borrowed from the technological world of computers and the language of so-called Information Technology)?

Then again, as Hylas admits, is not the supposed action of photons on the retina, like the supposed effect of vibrating air molecules on the ear, a form of *touch* and not sight? Last but not least, since our very perception of the *eye and brain themselves* (even through visual monitoring of so-called brainwave patterns on the screen of a technical instrument) is also, according to brain science itself, nothing but a hallucination created *by* the brain – how can what we visually perceive *as* an 'eye', 'retina', 'optic nerve', 'brain' or 'brain wave pattern' be in any way capable of 'explaining' our vision itself – or any other sense? If everything we perceive is 'all in the brain', then, as Berkeley already pointed out, does this not also apply to the brain itself – thus undermining the very foundation of 'brain science'?

It is through simple but basic questions such as these that Berkeley saw how the most basic and generally held assumptions of science breakdown through the simple logical principle of *reductio ad absurdum* – reducing themselves as they do to absurdities through their logical circularities.

All very well, say the physicists, but behind all that the brain conjures as sense perceptions, is nevertheless, something objectively real that they call 'energy' – whether in the form of light, conceived as electromagnetic energy, or the 'kinetic energy' of photons, atoms and molecules – which they claim are responsible (through no explanation they can offer) for all experiencing, whether of light, heat or sound – and this even though all conscious sensory experiencing is, by nature, essentially subjective ('in the mind' and not 'in the brain').

Berkeley himself had no intent to question or deny the *reality* of all that we perceive and experience. His only aim was to argue for the subjective rather than 'objective' or 'material' nature of experienced reality – its reality in consciousness – what he called 'mind', including the mind of God. The concept of 'energy' then, becomes the last line of defense by which to deny that everything, in Berkeley's terms, exists in the mind of God – the divine *nous* – and to deny also the essentially subjective nature of all reality. And if what is called 'energy', as well as 'matter', is, as it is thought to be, essentially insentient or *mindless*, Berkeley himself would no doubt have asked how can 'mind' – consciousness – in any possible way 'evolve' from, or be a product or property of it?

Today the concept of 'energy' serves as an attempt to replace a purely mechanistic model of the universe as 'matter in motion'. 'Sound' too, is thought of as 'matter in motion', which in turn is now considered a form of kinetic 'energy'. For this reason it is worthwhile to attend closely again to Berkeley's rigorous critique, through the figure of Philonous, of the whole idea that sound is reducible to motions of matter in the air:

Hylas: When the air is set into motion, we perceive a louder or softer sound in proportion to the air's motion; but when the air is still, we hear no sound at all.
Philonous: Granting that we never hear a sound except when some motion is produced in the air, I still don't see how you can infer from this that the sound itself is in the air.

Hylas: This motion in the external air is what produces in the mind the sensation of sound. By striking on the ear-drum it causes a vibration which is passed along the auditory nerves to the brain, whereon the mind experiences the sensation called sound.

Philonous: What! is sound a sensation?

Hylas: As I said: as perceived by us it is a particular sensation in the mind.

Philonous: And can any sensation exist outside the mind?

Hylas: No, certainly.

Philonous: But if sound is a sensation, how can it exist in the air, if by 'the air' you mean a senseless substance existing outside the mind?

Hylas: Philonous, you must distinguish sound as it is perceived by us from sound as it is in itself; or—in other words—distinguish the sound we immediately perceive from the sound that exists outside us. The former is indeed a particular kind of sensation, but the latter is merely a vibration in the air.

Philonous: I thought I had already flattened that distinction by the answer I gave when you were applying it in a similar case before. But I'll let that pass. Are you sure, then, that sound is really nothing but motion?

Hylas: I am.

Philonous: Whatever is true of real sound, therefore, can truthfully be said of motion.

Hylas: It may.

Philonous: So it makes sense to speak of motion as something that is loud, sweet, piercing, or grave?!

Hylas: I see you are determined not to understand me. Isn't it obvious that those qualities belong only to sensible sound or 'sound' in the ordinary everyday meaning of the word, but not to 'sound' in the real and scientific sense, which (as I have just explained) is nothing but a certain motion of the air?

Philonous: It seems, then, there are two sorts of sound—the common everyday sort that we hear, and the scientific and real sort that we don't hear.

Hylas: Just so.

Philas: And the latter kind of sound consists in motion.

Hylas: As I told you.

Philonous: Tell me, Hylas, which of the senses do you think the idea of motion belongs to? The sense of hearing?

Hylas: Certainly not. To the senses of sight and touch.

Philonous: It should follow then, according to you, that real sounds may possibly be seen or felt, but can never be heard.

Is there not an interesting parallel to be drawn here between the concept of sound as something that essentially inheres in vibratory motions of air – something which completely fails to explain our hearing of sounds *as* sounds – or as speech and music – and the idea, that light and colour are essentially nothing but an effect on the brain of motions of photons or electromagnetic waves at different 'energy levels' or purely quantitative 'frequencies'? For this no more explains our qualitative experience of light *as* light or colours *as* colours than the reduction of sounds to motions of air molecules explains our experience of sounds as sounds or music. It certainly does not explain our experience of the way music does indeed touch and move our *souls* and does not merely touch and set into vibration our ear drums or even our whole bodies. But then the very word 'soul' is one that the modern 'science' of 'psychology', despite its name does not even dare to touch!

For all these reasons the nature of 'qualia' – defined as basic sensory qualities such as colours and sounds – continues to vex today's philosophers of science, none of whom can even conceive of the idea, set out in my book entitled 'The Qualia Revolution', that consciousness or the soul is not a blank screen for receiving sensory impressions but has its own innately sensual qualities or 'qualia'. These 'soul qualities' are comparable to the felt qualities and moods of musical or vocal tones (warm or cool, light or heavy, bright or dark, rounded or sharp, hard or soft etc.) except that they are essentially tonal qualities of feeling awareness or 'soul' itself – what Seth calls "feeling tones". In other words, all outwardly perceived *sensory qualities* are the manifestation of *soul qualities* – understood as tonal qualities or 'qualia' of consciousness *as such* – 'the music of the soul' – and not as qualities of soul-less 'physical' objects.

All those sensory qualities of shape and form, sound and colour, hardness and softness, lightness and darkness, gravity and levity, warmth and coolness, flatness, sharpness and dullness etc. that we normally take as qualities of physical objects in the external world are the outward sensory expression of the same *soul qualities*, i.e. the same moods, tones and qualities of consciousness – of feeling awareness – from which *music* itself arises, communicating *through* this feeling awareness and not, as Berkeley so cogently argued, through mere vibrations of molecules of air.

Appendix 3

Towards a new Philosophy of Science and Religion: 'The Awareness Principle'

What I have termed 'The Awareness Principle' (abbreviated also to TAP) could be called a radical and highly original form of 'panpsychism' – or else subsumed under philosophical categories such as 'subjective idealism', 'immaterialism', 'transcendental phenomenology' and 'panentheism'. On the other hand, it is so original in conception that whilst its fundamental theses can be stated quite simply, these theses themselves make it different – in principle – from each and all previous varieties and formulations of the philosophical classifications referred to above. It is precisely this difference from previous forms of, for example, 'panpsychism' or 'subjective idealism', that grants the basic theses or principles of The Awareness Principle both their radicality and originality. Though each occasion in which, in this essay, I use the phrase 'in principle' constitutes in itself an important element of The Awareness Principle as such, to four of its most basic theses or principles of this Principle can be expressed as follows:

- All beings – everything that is – are distinct but inseparable portions and expressions of a universal consciousness field.
- Every being – everything that is – does not merely 'possess' some form of consciousness but is a distinct form or 'species' of consciousness in its own right.
- 'God' is not one being among others that happens to 'have' or 'possess' consciousness, indeed 'God' is not a being at all, but is nothing but consciousness as such (which in TAP is most often referred to as 'awareness').
- Consciousness as such ('awareness') possesses its own infinite, innate sensual qualities or 'qualia'. It is these innately sensual qualities of consciousness as such that find expression in all the sensory qualities or 'qualia' of perceptual phenomena and phenomenal experiencing.
- Reality is made up of fields, field patterns and field qualities of *awareness* and not of 'energy'.

Thesis 1 already introduces a radically new concept – that of the field character of consciousness or subjectivity. This is a concept that challenges the traditional identification of subjectivity with one or more localised 'subjects' of consciousness, as well as the traditional presupposition that consciousness or subjectivity is necessarily the property or function of such a 'subject', 'self', 'ego' or 'I'. What is described in TAP as a universal 'consciousness field' or 'field consciousness' is understood - in contrast to traditional notions of subjectivity and consciousness – as essentially a subjectivity or consciousness without a subject of consciousness (even a 'supreme' subject, or self, or being, in the form of what is called 'God' - see Thesis 3).

In contrast therefore to all previous forms of panpsychism, TAP does not merely take what is variously labelled 'mind', 'awareness' or 'consciousness' as an innate or even fundamental 'feature', 'property' or 'aspect' of all things – like some sort of inner kernel of consciousness surrounded by some 'physical' or 'material' carapace or taking some 'material' or 'physical' form. Instead it understands even the outer perceptual form of all things as forms that are not only perceived by and within consciousness, but as forms of consciousness in themselves. In other words, everything which we perceive and are conscious of is at the same time a distinct consciousness in its own right, both in form and content (see Theses 1 and 2). Here we come to a fundamental distinction between TAP and the 'subjective idealism' of Berkeley – who saw all perceptible things as 'ideas' in the 'mind' of God, rather than as distinct 'minds' or consciousnesses (plural) in their own right – all of them at the same time a distinct portion or expression of 'God', understood as a universal consciousness field or field consciousness. Put in other terms, the two most basic theses of The Awareness Principle can therefore be restated as follows:

1. **Awareness is everything – constitutive of all things or beings.**

2. **Everything** *is* **an individualised awareness or 'consciousness' in its own right, distinct but inseparable from others.**

We see here, how TAP removes all elements of psychophysical dualism from what is called 'panpsychism'. Instead it offers, like Berkeley, what can be called a wholly immaterialist 'monism' of awareness or consciousness – in contrast to both any form of neutral monism (one which does not say what 'the One' universal reality is) as well as a whole variety of dualisms, past and present. These include the dualism of 'subjects' and 'objects' of consciousness, of thought and extension (Descartes), of mind and matter, the psychic and the 'physical' – or of 'matter' and 'energy'. The new monism of awareness recognises the 'One' universal consciousness field as having infinite internal differentiations, portions and expressions – all of which are distinct but none of which are separable from the other - thus preserving its monistic character through an internal unity-in-multiplicity – the universal consciousness field or awareness being a field of what Michael Kosok called 'inseparable distinctions'.

Beyond current understandings of 'panpsychism'

The idea of consciousness as having a universal character is not a new one, and was re-suggested by philosopher David Chalmers in his TED talk, one in which he also admits to the possibility that consciousness may be a no less fundamental scientific 'datum' than, for example space, time and mass and that even photons might "have some element of raw subjective feeling". He adds that panpsychism "might seem crazy to us," he says, "but not to people from other cultures." What is interesting is how often he apologetically uses the term 'crazy' in reference to ideas associated with panpsychism. What is more significant philosophically, is that Chalmers in no way questions the conventional philosophical definition of 'panpsychism' as a view that everything "has" an element of 'mind', 'consciousness' or 'proto-consciousness' within it.

144

Hence the Stanford Encyclopaedia of Philosophy definition: "The word "panpsychism" literally means that everything has a mind." [my stress]. In contrast, Wikipedia's entry on panpsychism contradicts itself in the very first two sentences of its definition: "In philosophy, panpsychism is the view that consciousness, mind or soul (psyche) is a universal and primordial feature of all things. Panpsychists see themselves as minds in a world of mind." Later in the Wiki entry we find panpsychism defined "as a view that the universe has 'universal consciousness'" [my underlinings]

Here we come, no pun intended, to the crux of 'the matter'. For to see consciousness or 'mind' as a mere 'feature' of things or the universe as a whole is to reduce consciousness to some 'property' that they have or possess or that the universe as a whole has or possesses. This however, already implies a dualism between those 'things' or 'the universe', on the one hand, and the mind or consciousness that it 'has' on the other. This implicit dualism is negated by the second line of the Wiki definition: namely that "Panpsychists see themselves as minds in a world of mind."

Here there is no implicit dualism, but rather a 'mind only' philosophy of the sort associated with the 'subjective idealism' of Berkeley – as does the radical panpsychism of TAP, which indeed accepts fully that nothing exists except "minds in a world of mind".

The Awareness Principle as an *a priori* Principle

How The Awareness Principle may be argued – or argued against – as a principle is another 'matter'. Here it is useful to

145

briefly return to what Chalmers sees as the "crazy" idea that consciousness may be a fundamental scientific datum – a First Datum. Why "crazy"? I argue that it is self-evident in the most 'empirical' sense possible that the primary scientific fact or 'datum' is not the existence of a universe of beings or bodies in space-time but rather a (subjective) awareness or consciousness of such a universe. In all my writings on TAP however, I intentionally use singular impersonal phrases such as 'an awareness' or 'a consciousness'. I do so in order not to emphasise but to undermine the presupposition that when we talk of consciousness we are necessarily talking of a consciousness that is 'yours' or 'mine' or 'its', i.e. a mere property of a thing or being, self or 'subject'. Undermining this presupposition is actually critical to the whole logic by which I argue my position and spell out The Awareness Principle as a principle. One of many ways in which this principle can be stated is as follows:

Awareness (consciousness as such) cannot – in principle – be reduced to either a property or product of anything that there is already, a priori, an awareness of – whether this be a self or subject, ego, or 'I', or a being, body or brain.

It is an essential part of this principle that it rules out – in principle – any claim that the basic scientific or empirical datum is or can be simply a consciousness that is 'yours' or 'mine' – or in any way the private property of an individual self. Just as we cannot – in principle – even know of any body, thing, world or universe except through an a priori awareness of it, so also we cannot know of any self except through an a priori awareness of it. It is for this reason that – in principle – this very awareness cannot itself, be reduced to the private property of such a self. Similarly, since we also cannot even know of any thing or body except through an a priori awareness of it, it follows also that this very awareness cannot – in principle – be reduced in any way to a 'property' or 'product' of that thing or body.

Why any reductionist claim is, in contrast, a form of *reductio ad absurdum*, is something I argue using the analogy or example of dream consciousness. Thus any claim that consciousness as such is a property or product of any consciously perceived thing – such as the human brain for example – is as absurd, in principle, as claiming that dreaming or dream consciousness as such is a property or product of some one thing we happen to dream of, or to consciously perceive within a dream, i.e. within the larger field of our dream consciousness. Thus were we to dream of something with the form of the human brain, no philosopher or scientist would 'dream' of deducing that this single *dream*t phenomenon is the *cause* or 'explanation' of the dream as a whole, let alone all dreams or of dreaming as such. Yet this is precisely what reductionist brain science does when it takes a single phenomenon present within our waking consciousness – the human brain – as responsible for somehow 'producing' that consciousness. Nor, in the dream state, do we experience consciousness as something 'within' us – a basic assumption questioned in more depth later in this essay. On the contrary, the experience of dreaming, is phenomenologically, an experience of being within a dream, i.e. within a larger field of dream consciousness – one that embraces not only the dreamer but the entire dream environment and all that occurs or is perceived within it.

The Awareness Principle as a Phenomenological Principle

The Awareness Principle, with its emphasis on the field character of consciousness, can also be expressed not only in epistemological terms but also in phenomenological terms. As a fundamental phenomenological principle, The Awareness Principle can be stated as follows:

No *field* of consciousness can be explained as or reduced to the *property* or *product* of any *phenomenon or phenomena* experienced as present or emergent *within* that field.

Through recognising the field character of awareness, TAP undermines the reduction of awareness to either both 'subjects' or 'objects' of consciousness, replacing it instead with a dynamic of consciousness fields on the one hand, and the phenomena arising within and experienced within those fields on the other hand – each of these phenomena being no mere 'object' for a subject – but simply a form taken both by and within consciousness. This means also that all phenomena are but the perceptual form taken by different consciousnesses or 'minds' within the fields and field patterns of consciousness that define and constitute each other's consciousness. TAP is therefore what, in other works, I have called 'field-dynamic phenomenology'.

TAP versus Common Assumptions about Consciousness

We have already touched on a number of explicit or implicit assumptions that have tended to pervade and reoccur in all previous philosophies of mind or consciousness – including those described as forms of 'panpsychism' – and which find expression in the very language in which these philosophies tend to be couched. To fully understand the originality of The Awareness Principle it is important to recognise and be reminded of these assumptions:

1. The proprietorial assumption. This is the assumption that mind, consciousness – or a soul' or 'psyche' – is something that beings 'have' or 'possess' as their 'property', and this no matter whether we restrict this property to human beings or not. One of countless examples of this proprietorial language is that of Giordano Bruno: "There is nothing that does not <u>possess</u> a soul." [my stress]

2. Implicit dualism. The proprietorial assumption invariably implies a form of dualism, no matter whether this dualism is made explicit or argued for, or how it is named and defined. For wherever the proprietorial assumption is expressed through words such as 'have' or 'possess', a dualistic distinction is implied between whatever it is that is claimed to 'have or 'possess' consciousness and consciousness as such.

3. The very idea that consciousness is something in need of 'explanation', and that there is some "hard problem" here (Chalmers). This is actually one of the foundations of 'philosophy of mind'. Paradoxically however, it is the least questioned assumption of all. For if consciousness is truly a "First Datum" (Chalmers) then it is also precisely that which is

not in need of explanation at all - but rather that which offers the most fundamental and consistent source of explanations for all that is – for a 'Theory of Everything'. This is how consciousness is understood in The Awareness Principle – not as something in need of explanation but as the sole consistent and comprehensive source of explanation for everything else. The assumption that consciousness is something in need of 'explanation' also trips over itself in principle. For 'explanation' and 'explanatory' capacities and activities are, already and in themselves, activities of 'mind' or 'consciousness' – and therefore already assume and imply in advance the *a priori* reality of that which they seek to 'explain'. Yet if the reality of consciousness itself is a necessary presupposition and foundation of all 'explanation', then the very notion of 'explaining' consciousness becomes a circular one – for what is really being sought in the case of consciousness is not simply an 'explanation' of the sort, comparable say to an 'explanation' of the movements of the planets or stars, but an explanation of consciousness by and within an activity of consciousness, i.e. a type of explanation that derives from that which is to be explained. This is a very odd and circular sort of explanation or search for explanation indeed – since it is equivalent to seeking an explanation for the movement of planets and stars of a sort that, paradoxically, is itself a movement of those planets and stars – and therefore cannot, without circularity or paradox, 'explain' them at all. One might retort that there is no reason why consciousness should not come to an explanation of itself. But again, no explanation that is necessarily based – a priori – on what is to be explained can be claimed to be a post-hoc or a posteriori 'explanation' – which is how 'explanation' as such is usually understood.

4. The assumption that consciousness is 'within' us. What if, in reality, it is the other way round: namely that we are within consciousness – understood as a field of awareness, that like space itself, embraces not just our internal thoughts and feelings but the entire world we perceive around us and everything in it? Indeed what if what we perceive as the empty space around us and other things in the world is essentially a spatial field of consciousness? This is what I argue. As for the modern 'within us' model of consciousness, this is no better represented than by the fashionable neuroscientific reduction of consciousness to a function of the brain - something within our own skull. Hardly a day goes by without images of a brain housed within a skull appearing in some popular journalistic article, and/or some new mapping of brain areas through hi-tech instrumentation – all of which, of course show no more than a 'correlation' of these with different states of consciousness and no causal relation at all. Yet even before the modern fad for brain science arose, we were all taught that sensory perception was a result of information (for example in the form of wavelengths of sound or light) being received by our sense organs and then piped through nerve channels to the brain. No one seems to have noticed the new twist given to this model by modern neuroscience, which argues that the brain using this information then creates and projects out a picture of the world. In other words it is seriously assumed (whether this assumption be

implicit or explicitly stated – as it is by Anil Seth) that our brains actively hallucinate our own outer, external world.

5. Yet if this is the case, what is effectively being claimed is that the brain can receive and interpret sensory information from objects in the world (for example through light emanated by or reflected off them) even though these objects are then agreed to be nothing but subjective hallucinations created by the brain! In other words, the brain interprets 'sensory data' coming from imagined or hallucinated objects in its own hallucinated sensory world. Another absurd implication of this model of perception is that, in the last analysis, the only 'real' sensory object is the brain itself – which, for some unstated reason is, according to brain science, the only object of perception that is not a hallucination – and can therefore be dissected or electronically scanned in brain labs!

This pseudo-scientific philosophy might as well be called 'pan-brainism' – for it effectively replaces the panpsychic principle that we are minds or consciousnesses living within a world of mind or consciousness with the principle that we are just brains living within a world of (and created by) brains. This philosophy is then hailed as a great scientific achievement of 'brainy' neuroscientists (albeit with the help of their brain's own hallucinated neuroscientific instruments and scanning technologies!) rather than being immediately dismissed as philosophically absurd and brainless pseudo-science. Another twist in the tail of this tall story of the brain is that it ends up accepting that the brain itself exists in a world of consciousness and consciously perceived objects – albeit a hallucinatory world supposedly 'created' by the brain through information coming to it from that world. One is reminded here of Hindu and Buddhist philosophies which declare the world beheld by and within consciousness to be an illusion, and Brahman the sole unchanging reality. Now we are asked by neuroscience to replace 'Brahman' with 'Brain' or 'Brainman' and to recognise that organ we perceive as the brain to be the only object that is not an illusion or hallucination i.e. not an imagined – or even a real perceptual phenomenon – as perceived within a field of consciousness.

6. The causality assumption. The scientific attempt to 'explain' consciousness suggests also some form of causal explanation i.e. some way of explaining how consciousness is or maybe 'caused' by something other than consciousness. But what if consciousness itself, is, in principle, an a-causal domain and a field of a-causal relations? This would render all causal explanation of this field contradictory. There is nothing mysterious about the notion of *a-causal* relations. If two things, an armchair and a table, say are co-present in space, we see no need to seek some causal explanation of the presence of the armchair in the presence of the table or vice versa. I have already alluded to the idea that space itself is nothing objective but a spatial field of consciousness. By this I mean a field of consciousness in which things can be perceived as both distinct and co-present (like a table and armchair). Clearly no contents of space – no things within it – can even be perceived or distinguished without a space in which to distinguish them, i.e. without space as such. Similarly no contents of consciousness - nothing we are conscious of – can be distinguished except within a spatial field of consciousness. Space is essentially a

field of presence or co-presence of things within awareness. More specifically it is co-presence within a field of consciousness, a co-presence which implies no causal relations between those things. Consciousness, as space, is that which makes it possible for things to stand out or 'ex-ist' within it. But a field of consciousness is also more than just a field of presence or even co-presence in which things like tables and chairs just 'stand' there. A field of consciousness is also a field of *a-causal* interaction and interrelatedness. If we see two dogs or children playing or two people interacting in any way we do not assume that what one dog, child or person does is caused by the other. The phenomenon that is now present to and within consciousness is not any sort of causally related chain of events or actions but a form of a-causal and reciprocal *inter-action* - a form of dynamic interrelatedness. This brings us to two further fundamental principles of what I call 'field-dynamic phenomenology' – the essential philosophy of TAP as a new form of panpsychism:

1. **No two phenomena present within or emergent from a field of consciousness can be said to 'cause' one another.**

2. **All phenomena present within or emergent from a field of consciousness are inwardly and a-causally connected with one another through that field and by virtue of having a common origin in it.**

The Awareness Principle as an Ontological Principle

In the context of the history of philosophy, Heidegger's shift from a new phenomenological epistemology to a 'fundamental ontology' focussed on Being followed from his rejection of the

154

entire phenomenological language of 'subjectivity'. This rejection was rooted in the fact that he saw within the language of Husserl's phenomenology a continued retention of the old metaphysical subject-object dualism. What Heidegger did not see however, was that this dualism was predicated on the old assumption – challenged for the first time by TAP – that subjectivity as such is necessarily the property, function or activity of some form of 'subject', whether 'empirical' or 'transcendental'. As a result he placed the question of the nature and essence of Being - rather than the question of consciousness - as the most primordial philosophical question of all, i.e. *the question of why there is anything at all, rather than nothing and what it means for anything at all to 'be'*. In contrast, The Awareness Principle recognises that 'The Question of Being' - can itself only arise through a primordial *awareness* of Being. We ourselves only know that we *are* through this primordial awareness of Being. Similarly we only know of the existence or Being of any thing or being through an awareness of it. It is precisely for this reason that this very awareness (i.e. consciousness as such) cannot – in principle – be reduced either to the private property of any beings, (including human beings) it is aware of or to the product of any thing or body, (including the human body and brain).

On the contrary, all experienced bodies and beings are but more or less individualised embodiments and portions of an unbounded and trans-personal awareness field – manifest to and experienced by each other within that field. In other words, all that exists is indeed 'minds within a world of mind'.

Note on the author

Born in London in 1952, Peter Wilberg studied philosophy at Magdalen College Oxford and holds an MA in Humanistic Psychology. He has spent his life researching and writing on the philosophy of science and religion, medicine and psychiatry, psychology and psychotherapy and is the author of 25 books on these and other subjects, His other published books include *The Awareness Principle – a radical new philosophy of life, science and religion; The Illness is the Cure – an introduction to Life Medicine,* and *The QUALIA Revolution – from quantum physics to Cosmic Qualia Science.* Further books and essays by Peter Wilberg can be found on his Amazon Author Page and on his multiple websites. For links to these see his homepage: www.peterwilberg.org

Bibliography

Avery, Samuel *The Dimensional Structure of Consciousness – a physical basis for immaterialism* Compari 1995

Balint, Michael *The Doctor, His Patient and the Illness* Churchill Livingstone

Berkeley, George *Three Dialogues between Hylas and Philonous*

Buber, Martin *The Eclipse of God* Humanities Press International 1988

Dahlin, Bo *The Ontological Reversal: A Figure of Thought of Importance for Science Education* Department of Educational Sciences, Karlstad University, Sweden

Frankl, Victor *The Will to Meaning* Touchstone 1984

Eagleton, Terry *The Gospels* Verso 2007

Gendlin, Eugene *Experiencing and the Creation of Meaning* Northwestern University Press 1997

Heidegger, Martin *The Question Concerning Technology* Harper Torchbooks 1977

Heidegger, Martin *Introduction to Metaphysics*

Heidegger, Martin *What is Called Thinking?* Harper Torchbooks 1968

Heidegger, Martin *Zollikon Seminars* Northwestern University Press 2001

Hogan, James P. *Kicking the Sacred Cow: Heresy and Impermissible Thoughts in Science* Mass Market Paperbacks

Husserl, Edmund *The Crisis of the European Sciences and Transcendental Philosophy* Northwestern University Press, 1970

Illich, Ivan *Medical Nemesis; The Expropriation of Health* Penguin 1990

Jones, Roger *Physics as Metaphor* Abacus, 1983

Lewontin, R.C. *Biology as Ideology, the doctrine of DNA* Harper 1993

Roberts, Jane Seth *Speaks, The Eternal Validity of the Soul*

Roberts, Jane *The Universe as Idea Construction*

Tauber, Alfred *The Immune Self: Theory or Metaphor?* Cambridge University Press 1997

Tennenbaum, Jonathan *Power vs. Energy - The Difference Between Dynamis and Energeia* Executive Intelligence Review November 22, 2002 issue

Wilberg, Peter *The Awareness Principle – a radical new philosophy of life, science and religion* New Yoga Publications 2007

Wilberg, Peter *Event Horizon* New Yoga Publications 2013

Wilberg, Peter *Heidegger, Medicine and 'Scientific Method'; The Unheeded Heritage of the Zollikon Seminars* New Gnosis Publications 2003

Wilberg, Peter *Heidegger, Phenomenology and Indian Thought* New Yoga Publications

Wilberg, Peter *The Illness IS the Cure, an introduction to Life Medicine and Life Doctoring – a new existential approach to medicine* 2nd extended edition, New Yoga Publications 2014

Wilberg, Peter Wilberg *The QUALIA Revolution; From Quantum Physics to Cosmic Qualia Science* New Gnosis Publications 2004

Zigmond, David *If you want good personal healthcare – see a vet* New Gnosis Publications, 2015

www.ingramcontent.com/pod-product-compliance
Lightning Source LLC
LaVergne TN
LVHW051103080426
835508LV00019B/2037